Wolverine
PUBLISHING

By Jonathan Thesenga
Photos: Ben Moon

WARNING:

Rock climbing is a dangerous activity. The publisher and author assume no responsibility for injury or death resulting from the use of this book.

The information in this book is unverified and the authors and publisher cannot guarantee its accuracy. Assessments of the difficulty and risk of climbs are based on opinions and are entirely subjective. No climb is "safe"—you can be injured or killed attempting any climb in this book. Please take all precautions and use your own ability, evaluation, and judgement to assess the risks of a particular climb, rather than relying on the information in this book. This book is not intended as an instructional manual. If you are unsure of your ability to handle any circumstances that may arise, seek professional instruction or employ the services of a professional guide.

THE AUTHORS AND PUBLISHER MAKE NO REPRESENTATIONS OR WARRANTIES, EXPRESSED OR IMPLIED, OF ANY KIND REGARDING THE CONTENTS OF THIS BOOK, AND EXPRESSLY DISCLAIM ANY REPRESENTATION OR WARRANTY REGARDING THE ACCURACY OR RELIABILITY OF INFORMATION CONTAINED HEREIN. THE USER ASSUMES ALL RISK ASSOCIATED WITH THE USE OF THIS BOOK.

Wolverine PUBLISHING

For more information about Wolverine Publishing, please call 970-984-2815, email dave@wolverinepublishing.com, or visit us on the web at www.wolverinepublishing.com.

FRONT COVER:
Mike Stoger on *Kings of Rap* 5.12d (page 30)
Photography: Ben Moon, Moonphoto.

TITLE PAGE:
Sonnie Trotter on *East Face of Monkey Face* 5.13d (page 66)
Photography: Ben Moon, Moonphoto.

Printed in China.

INTERNATIONAL STANDARD BOOK NUMBER:
ISBN-10: 0-9721609-6-5
ISBN-13: 978-0-9721609-6-4

LIBRARY OF CONGRESS CATALOG IN PUBLICATION DATA:
Library of Congress Control Number: 2006923905

WORDS:
Jonathan Thesenga.

PHOTOGRAPHY:
All action shots by Ben Moon, Moonphoto, unless otherwise credited. Cliff shots Jonathan Thesenga and Dave Pegg.

PUBLISHED BY:
Wolverine Publishing
5439 County Rd 243
New Castle
CO 81647 USA

Photo: Damon Corso

URBANCLIMBER.TV
MAGAZINE

www.urbanclimbermag.tv **IS THE NEW FREE**
CLIMBING FILM AND VIDEO NETWORK

- SICKEST FOOTAGE
- UPLOAD YOUR OWN VIDEOS

CONTENTS

MAD ROCK

100% pure SCIENCE FRICTION

FOREWORD

By Brooke Sandahl

For years I'd driven straight past Smith Rock, opting for the quality, sun drenched, crystalline rocks of California. Surely there couldn't be real routes lurking in and amongst all that choss. However, after viewing a friend's slides one evening, I became convinced that there was indeed quality product to be had.

In 1983, after a failed attempt on the north face of Mt Redoubt and ensuing epic bivy, which left my back totally crook, I found myself nursing along the trail towards the Dihedrals for my first look at the Park. When I reached the base of the Heinous/Darkness wall, unable to straighten up, I cocked my head to the right and through one eye caught my first glimpse of Smith Rock. Astounded, I traced a line of micro-edges and pockets ascending ever skyward. Jaw dropped, I shuffled forward a few steps and *Chain Reaction* came into view. It looked like a triple-crested orange wave—crisp, clean cut and stunningly hard to climb! Having toured many of the best climbing areas throughout the West and the Rocky Mountains, I knew what the hard climbs looked and felt like (most were pure crack lines). Those routes didn't bear any resemblance to what I was seeing. At the time the hardest routes in Josh were 20 to 30 feet tall—the Darkness at Noon wall was easily five times as long, looming large, a vast two-dimensional wasteland with nary a hold to be seen.

The first touch of stone at a new crag is always a momentous occasion, generally very telling, and allowing a glimpse into the future. Oftentimes this is a moment that brings one psych and fills the heart with pure adrenaline. Gently placing my fingers into a miniscule, sharp-edged tuft pocket and simultaneously attempting to eyeball the summit anchor miles away, the only thing this place was telling me was: "You're screwed. Pack the bags punter and head back to where you came from." Despite an overwhelming sense of inadequacy and doom, my next thought was: I'm moving here!

A year later I had returned, installed in Bend's westside. My first day back at the crag, I trolled the empty park looking to hookup with a belay and sample the goods. The very first person I met was obviously one of the resident hardmen, Chris Grover. Unfiltered Camel cigarette in hand, The Grove gave me the run down on the Smith scene. I mentioned to Chris about a local named Alan Watts whom I'd read about in Climbing Magazine's Basecamp section.

"Yeah, Alan's the real deal," said The Grove. "He's the one pushing lines up all these blank faces." He also told me that Alan was going to COCC (local community college) as a cover to keep the rent-paying parents placated, but in fact was climbing fulltime and looking for someone to climb with mid-week.

Loading into Alan's burnt-orange Datsun B-210 became a ritual that spring. Knee deep in junk-food wrappers, we wore ruts in Highway 97 going between town and the Park. We always made the ritual stop in Terrebonne, at Ferguson's Market, to load up on Snickers bars and M&Ms. A small town kid from Madras, Alan Watts was one of the nicest people you could ever hope to meet. He exhibited a mischievous sense of humor, was quick of wit, and was one of the singularly most focused (on climbing) people I'd ever known. Additionally, he was an avid new router and technically brilliant climber who possessed the unique ability to always find the hardest possible sequence on any given route.

It was a magic time, learning to pull on the welded tuff pockets and crimps, following Big Al on project after project, and getting to know and climb with the small tight-knit group of locals. One quickly learns that a thug's approach doesn't work at Smith. Learning the requisite technique and proper footwork is imperative if you want to succeed on the harder lines. As contact strength improved and the mind strengthened, proper climbing style evolved; the impossible-looking lines started to feel climbable.

It wasn't all business in those days. Back then the tourists would always park in the first lot. The climbers would continue past into the next lot, which was usually empty. We each had our own parking spot (sometimes even writing our names in chalk on the appropriate stall). It was an unwritten rule to keep

AND THEN ... Brooke on the FA of *Da Kine Corner* in 1987. Photo Greg Epperson.

"Behind [Mike Volk's] trailer, tucked in among the juniper trees, was a full Camp Four style outdoor gym ... " Local training psychos Grover (left) and Watts work out. Photo Brooke Sandahl.

these stalls open and woe to he who should inadvertently take one of our spots. A proper warm up is key before vigorous pocket pulling, and we had many methods. Sometimes Alan would bring tennis rackets and we'd lay a climbing rope across the road for a net and practice our ground strokes, other times we'd bust the skates out and practice our best Rodney Mullen street-style tricks and curb grinds to the latest hardcore tunes. There was always the informal club house at Mike Volk's across the street. Behind the trailer, tucked in among the juniper trees, was a full Camp Four style outdoor gym, complete with Bacher ladder, slack wire, various primitive wooden edges to hang from, free weights, and various other training gizmos. The Special Olympics (as we referred to them) often carried on down to the park, where there was the official first joint finger edge (one arm hangs only/timed) located in the "Office" (Heinous/Darkness corner), the pain-tolerance tester, a finger wrenching jam in a flat ceiling (also timed), and of course rock throwing championships, which were always very competitive.

One of the great beauties of Smith in those days was the total lack of authoritarian rule. In the first ten years of climbing at Smith, I never once saw a ranger cross the bridge over the Crooked River. In essence, once over the bridge, we were the ruling force and did as we damn well pleased. Being located in the

heart of the Wild West meant we were free to trundle, bolt, shoot, swing, wire-walk, and do anything our imaginations could think up. There was a time when I'd bring the "old gauge" down to the park. It was a rusty Mossberg single shot 12 gauge. Broken down, it fit neatly inside my tall crag pack and was undetectable. Scott Franklin loved that thing. We'd head up into the Aggro Gully and blast a pigeon or sassy varmint. It made a lovely sound echoing off the canyon walls and down towards the river. Once, when I was out with Scott and Jerry Moffatt, a startled pigeon rocketed skyward, casually Uncle Jerry tracked and dropped it with the nonchalance of a British nobleman. Other times, as an unsuspecting friend neared a redpoint crux, we'd let the Mossberg roar—generally it was enough thwart all but the most concentrated of efforts. Sadly the Mossberg collects mainly rust these days, but it's tempting to bring it back down to the Dihedrals and thin the herd a little in these more crowded times. Other flagrant violations of the law included one very well known climber's efforts at the big dope grow. Sadly, he wasn't a horticulturalist and the whole lot turned out to be bunk! He marched down to the Dihedrals one day with a bulging Kelty Expedition pack on his back and a huge garbage bag in each hand. Puzzled looks ensued, until he emptied the contents and the laughter erupted. He then proceeded to torch the lot in an impressive bonfire at the base of *Heinous Cling.*

The end of the year climbing party was quite a tradition in those days. Typically held at the end of October or beginning of November, when the big Pacific low-pressure systems began to dominate the weather patterns. Normally a pretty healthy crew— this was the one event everybody came to ready to hammer down. Contests were arranged (with cash prizes) and sometimes the competition was fierce. The contests were pretty simple: The mountaineering contest consisted of those who could keep their feet in a bucket of ice water longest. Another was first to puke. At one party, Kent Benesch slyly took home the money by stealing a can of Campbell's Chunky Soup from the kitchen and blorting it out in a faux puke! Karma would later visit Kent on the drive home in a friend's new car. The pull-up contest was usually the biggest event. The 1986 party had special significance as it pitted local training psycho Chris Grover vs. French heavyweight J.B. Tribout. JB's tear through the park that fall was legendary—with first ascents of *Rude Boys* and the coveted *To Bolt or Not to Be* (first 5.14 in America). Both well liquored, but ready to compete, they each stepped up to the bar with their game faces on. The mighty Grove banged out an impressive number; however J.B. rose to the occasion and with the crowd chanting, topped it by another twenty. The crowd went wild and J.B spinning from the effort celebrated with a double-fisted pump. Looking up at his profusely bleeding knuckles, (the bar had been set too close to a rough-sawn wooden beam) all he could do was laugh and toss back another shooter.

I've always liked my friend Jim Birdwell's definition of rules for climbing. Rule number one: There are no rules! I think this attitude is very applicable to the formative years at Smith. Of course we had a strict code of ethics and an unspoken set of rules, but we did things our way (a natural and rational evolution) and certainly never pushed it on anyone else. We were unconcerned about how we were "supposed to do it," and instead of squabbling, we just went climbing. Generally we had the last laugh, as the loud-mouthed visiting hard guy spouting ethics and slagging us off as mere sport climbers, was usually paddled hard on the entry level 5.12s and sent home tail between legs. Although Smith Rock has been dubbed the birthplace of American sport climbing, it is in my estimation a convenient and contrived title. Many people forget (or never knew) the true history and tradition of many Smith

Watts (left) and Grover psych up for *Rambo Roof*. Photo Brooke Sandahl.

routes. Smith was originally a crack climbing area. It wasn't until most of the crack lines were exhausted that people started venturing onto the blank faces. Even then natural gear was used where it could be placed and bolts were a last resort. Unfortunately, many of these bold routes have become sanitized by retro bolting. It saddens me to see the heritage and tradition of these extremely proud routes probably lost forever. *Heinous Cling* was once protected by a row of RPs, cams, and a few interspersed bolts. It was a serious undertaking and running it out for the anchor, on cams stuffed in the big hole, gave one pause for reflection. Will I go for fifty if I pump off the final moves? Will the cams hold? Other routes like the classic *Firing Line/Power Dive* have lost a lot of their former glory through retro bolting. Yes, the moves are the same, but the experience isn't. Now many of the new routes sport "runouts" with the last bolt at knee level while you're clipping the next. This degradation of the climbing experience slaps the faces of those who went before. On a more positive note, some of the new generation are becoming hip to the style and ethics of an ascent. Traditionally placed gear ascents like Sonnie Trotter's recent climb of the Monkey's *East Face* hopefully will serve as an example for coming generations.

Eventually the world became hip to Smith Rock and the vacuum was broken. Alan's stunning *Chain Reaction* photo on the cover of Mountain Magazine did much to alert the rest of the global climbing community to Smith's whereabouts. As the international hardcore started to arrive another era was ushered in. The real education for us locals was to take a quantum leap forward, make new friendships, exchange ideas, and enmesh contrasting cultures.

Brooke H Sandahl **March 2006**

Wolverine
PUBLISHING

INTRODUCTION

Smith Rock has over a *thousand* routes—and that's the problem. Many of these routes are total piles that should never have been climbed in the first place. The last thing you want to do is waste your time or get yourself freaked out on some jingus pitch. Enter *Smith Rock Select,* the tome you're currently holding.

First though, a caveat: If you want to know about every single route that's ever been climbed at Smith—don't buy this book. Alan Watts is the godfather of Smith and has written the bible to the area, *A Climber's Guide To Smith Rock*, replete with interesting history, personal humor, and intricate hand-drawn topos. An updated edition of Alan's book should be available soon.

Smith Rock Select, on the other hand, is far from exhaustive in its coverage. In fact, it's exactly what its name implies: a guide to the sweetest pitches at Smith, with color photos and detailed up-to-date route descriptions.

So buy the damn book, enjoy the park, leave your dog at home, avoid the sun, climb the Monkey, swap beta for *Churning*, pimp and crimp nubbins, wait in line at *Heinous*, go to the backside and ditch the crowds, look up in awe at *To Bolt*, bitch about the hike out, watch the sunset over Asterisk Pass, and last, but not least, drink a beer (or four) at the Terrebonne Depot and pore over this guidebook, ticking off the day's climbs and planning for tomorrow's.

—Jonathan Thesenga

ESSENTIAL BETA

Getting to Smith Rock State Park

Erupting from the high desert of Central Oregon, the volcanic tuff cliffs of Smith Rock are about three hours southeast of the Rose City, Portland, 25 minutes from the onetime logging town and now Californicated boutique city of Bend, 10 minutes from the traffic-light congestion hell of Redmond, and three minutes (average speed 35.2 mph without stopping for the train) from the uber-chic farming community of Terrebonne.

The closest airport is a tiny municipal set-up in Redmond; there are several daily puddle-jumper flights from Portland and Salt Lake City. There are four car rental agencies at the airport. If you can't afford a car rental or your driving record is so jacked no one will rent even a donkey to you, call me and I'll drive you out to the crag for $450—one way, plus gas.

Getting to Smith Rock is ridiculously simple: If you get lost, just look for the giant walls off to the north—that's Smith. At the single flashing yellow light in Terrebonne turn east onto Smith Rock Way. From the turn it's three miles to the park. Cross the train tracks, and at the bottom of the hill turn left onto NE 1st Street, which will eventually turn into Wilcox Ave. After a couple of miles take a left at Crooked River Drive where there's a State Park sign pointing you towards Smith Rock. For climbing at Smith Rock proper, park at the main area, but if you're going to the Northern Point or west side of the Lower Gorge continue driving to the end of the road to park.

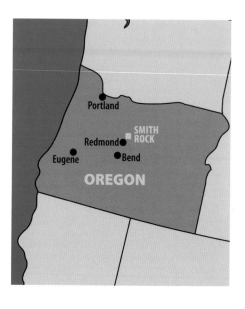

When to Visit

You can climb at Smith year-round (and most people do) but the summer months are brutally hot (I'm talking 90-plus degrees by 10 a.m.) requiring you to chase the shade the entire day (which isn't difficult thanks to the east-west aspect of the park's climbing) but it does limit what you can climb. If you have been dreaming of sending *Chain Reaction*, don't show up in August—when that sucker (as well as 90-percent of the frontside climbing) bakes in the sun longer than the Hawaiian Tropic Tanning Team.

The primo climbing season for ticking hard routes at Smith is short, typically late fall through early spring. The winter weather can be fickle, sometimes dipping into the sub-30s during the day with snow, sleet, and other jingus forms of frozen precipitation. However, some of the best days at Smith can be had mid-winter when it's 45 degrees and the sun warms the stone to perfect redpoint temps. Rain is rarely a factor as the Cascade Range to the west blocks most of the heavy rain that Oregon is infamous for.

DRIVING TIMES
(all times personally driven and certified by author)

Terrebonne: 3 minutes

Seattle: 7 hours

Boise: 6 hours

San Francisco: 9 hours

Salt Lake City: 12 hours

Las Vegas: 17 hours

Denver: 21 hours

Omaha: 23 hours

Minneapolis: 26 hours

Dallas: 30 hours

Chicago: 31 hours

Philadelphia: 42 hours

New York City: 43 hours

Miami: 48 hours

Mexico City: a really long time

FRONTSIDE AREAS

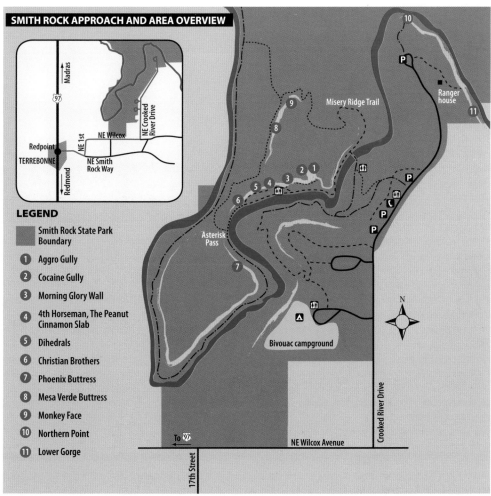

SMITH ROCK APPROACH AND AREA OVERVIEW

LEGEND

Smith Rock State Park Boundary

1. Aggro Gully
2. Cocaine Gully
3. Morning Glory Wall
4. 4th Horseman, The Peanut, Cinnamon Slab
5. Dihedrals
6. Christian Brothers
7. Phoenix Buttress
8. Mesa Verde Buttress
9. Monkey Face
10. Northern Point
11. Lower Gorge

Paul Gardner and Connor Eddy gearing up at the Dihedrals.
Photo Stacey Eddy.

Parking

That funky yellow box at the main parking area? Yeah, that's where you pay the $3 to park your vehicle at Smith. Don't for a second think about skating on paying the fee—you're guaranteed to come back from your super-sick sendfest in the Dihedrals to find a lovely parking violation ticket on your windshield. You can also pay $25 for a 12-month pass. The math whizzes out there will be able to figure out that if you plan on visiting Smith more then nine times throughout a 12-month period, it makes sense to throw down the $25 for the pass.

Dogs

Technically your dog is allowed at Smith Rock—you just have to keep it on a leash at all times or face a stout $94 ticket. Here's the catch, though: Your dog must always be under your "physical control," meaning you can't tie it up while you climb. Yes, that's right. You have to physically hold onto your dog's leash even while you belay. And the leash can be no longer than six feet. Seriously! People have been ticketed for having their dog tied up to their pack that's two-feet away or having too long of a leash.

The best advice is to leave your dog at home. Smith Rock is simply not a place to bring your dog. Not only is dealing with Fido while you climb a pain in the ass, but it's also a pain in the ass for everyone else at the crag. Smith is dusty and crowded enough without some hyper mutts turning the scene into an annoying mess of dirt and noise. Believe it our not, not every single person thinks your dog is "cutesy wootsey" or enjoys hearing some spazzy-assed mutt barking its brains out. Do everyone a favor and leave your dog in the yard at home and enjoy a canine-free day at the crag. (And, no, I'm not a dog hater. I have a dog, and love her so much I never bring her to Smith to sit around in the dirt and heat.)

Where to Stay

There are two camping options. First there is **the walk-in campground at the park**, which costs $4 a night, per person (that price includes your daily parking fee). Located 50 yards before the main parking area and overlooking the entire crag, the campground is super convenient and ultra scenic. You can get jacked up on coffee while watching the sunrise hit the walls and then, a few hours later, kick back with some beers as you admire the sunset. Fires and RVs are not allowed and you can't sleep in the back of your truck or van, but there are nice bathrooms and showers. It's a self-pay set-up, but don't try and skip out on kicking down the cash because the campground host and park employees are vigilent on enforcing the fee and patrol the area multiple times each day.

The second camping choice is **Skull Hollow Campground**, or as it is more commonly known, "The Grasslands," located 7.9 miles from Smith. The camping here is free, making it a serious consideration if you plan on being at Smith for a while. Water is not available, but fires are allowed and there are a couple of pit toilets. To get there, get back on the main road (Wilcox Ave.) heading east, and at the first main junction continue heading east on Lone Pine Road. Soon after the junction you'll cross the Crooked River, and the road will angle north. Take a left at the Gray Butte Trailhead turnoff and almost immediately you'll see the campground sign on your left.

If roughing it ain't your gig, there are numerous hotels and motels in Redmond and Bend, ranging from $200-a-night executive suites to by-the-hour fleabag dives.

We understand...

Your climbing wall needs.

Food and Gear

There are countless chain restaurants, pseudo-chic eateries, pub-and-grubs, pretentious wine and martini bars, coffee houses, burger-and-fry holes, and taco shacks throughout Terrebonne, Redmond, and Bend, but for post-climbing food there is only one place to go: the climber owned and operated **Terrebonne Depot** (541-548-5030), just west of the train tracks at 400 NW Smith Rock Way on your way into the park. Housed in the old train station (thus the name), Terrebonne Depot has the full run of quality food and drink at reasonable prices. Plus, if you ever need any beta, owners and Smith turbo-locals Ian and Kristen Yurdin can dial you in on just about any route in the park.

For quick-hit groceries and a taste of the local central Oregon farmer vibe, be sure to visit Ferguson's Mini-Mart and Gas Station on Highway 97 in Terrebonne. For a more complete grocery selection head north 100 yards to Albertsons (aka "The Bert") or rally into Redmond where there's a Safeway and Grocery Outlet, among other options.

Between Fergusons and The Bert, right on the corner to Smith, is **Redpoint Climbers Supply** (800-923-6207). They have the full quiver of gear you'll need from chalk to draws to shoes. In Bend, check out **Mountain Supply** (541-388-0688) at 834 NW Colorado Avenue, which also has an equipment rental service. If you need a guide for a day, weekend, week, or more, you can arrange one through **First Ascent Climbing Services** (800-325-5462) at Redpoint Climbers Supply. If you want your kid to learn more at summer camp than how to smoke weed through an apple, First Ascent also offers climbing camps as well. You can check out Redpoint and First Ascent on the web at: www.goclimbing.com.

For more Beta, plus news and new route updates visit the local climbing website www.smithrock.com.

Other Climbing Options

If the weather does turn nasty at Smith, you can venture into Bend and get your pump on at **Inclimb Gym** (www.inclimb.com, 541-388-6764). Inclimb is a great facility with mostly bouldering but some top roping and leading is possible. For $12 per person you can boulder until your forearms burst. Call the crew over there any time after noon and they'll give you directions to the gym.

If you just gotta scratch that bouldering itch, there's some great local bouldering around Bend, Sisters, and Prineville. For directions and beta, stop off at Redpoint in Terrebonne or Inclimb in Bend.

TERREBONNE DEPOT
FOOD + DRINK

Serving Fresh, Local, Organic
- Salads
- Homemade Pizzas
- Buffalo Burgers
- Fish Tacos
- Steaks and Pastas
- Creative Vegitarian Options
- Kids Menu

ESPRESSO, BEER, WINE & COCKTAILS

DECK W/ OUTDOOR SEATING

SMITH ROCK AND CASCADE VIEWS

541.548.5030

LOCATED IN THE HISTORIC
TERREBONNE TRAIN DEPOT

400 NW Smith Rock Way, Terrebonne
(1/4 mile East off Hwy 97 toward Smith Rock State Park)

Lisa Hensel on *Toxic* 5.11b (page 23).

1
AGGRO GULLY

Sport climbers rejoice—your salvation from the damnation of Smith's slabs is here. The Aggro Gully is all about steep powerful climbing, where power and strong fingers can make up for that lack of technical face-climbing finesse, oh so brutally and embarrassingly exposed in the Dihedrals. If hard, steep redpoints are your gig, this is your zone.

The Aggro Gully (much like the Arsenal at Rifle) was long dismissed as choss, until a handful of climbers began "aggro-cleaning" the rock, shedding the wall of its loose flakes and rotten junk. The result? Smith's highest concentration of 5.13s and 5.14s, all of them steep, powerful, well bolted, and outstanding. Sure there might be a smattering of "no-way-Mother-Nature-made-this" pockets and a fair amount of glue, but, ultimately, these black eyes do little to detract from the gully's beautiful climbing.

Since the gully is cloaked in shade for most of the day (it doesn't get any sun until early afternoon, and even then it's only for two or three hours), it's not uncommon to score prime redpoint temps while the rest of Smith is broiling. The only time of year when the gully is completely out of condition is winter, when the stone never gets enough sun to warm up.

As with the Churning Buttress, locals have all these routes completely sussed, either from running laps on them (e.g. *The Quickening* and *Aggro Monkey*) or from working them into submission as multi-season projects (e.g. *Bad Man, White Wedding,* and *Villain*), so you won't be wanting for crux beta. Most of the routes are equipped with fixed draws, adding to the climbing-gym vibe.

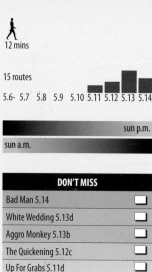

12 mins

15 routes

5.6- 5.7 5.8 5.9 5.10 5.11 5.12 5.13 5.14

sun p.m.

sun a.m.

DON'T MISS	
Bad Man 5.14	☐
White Wedding 5.13d	☐
Aggro Monkey 5.13b	☐
The Quickening 5.12c	☐
Up For Grabs 5.11d	☐
Toxic 5.11b	☐

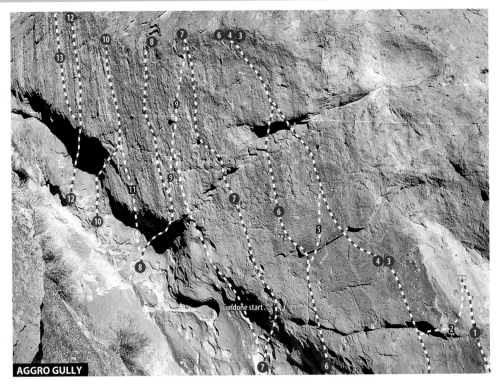

AGGRO GULLY

❶ Highway To Hell 5.12a ★
The easiest route on the wall! Too bad it's marginal, especially compared to the impressive lines to its left. More often than not this route is only partially climbed when trying the next two 5.14 link-ups.

❷ Repeat Offender 5.14a ★★
Dives off *Highway To Hell* after the third bolt, tackles a severe section of climbing, connects into *Villain*, and then shoots back to *Highway's* anchors. Not a very impressive line, but, hey, it's 14a and that's really all that matters right?

❸ Shock and Awe 5.14c ★★★★
(aka It's Not a Link-Up)
A carpet-bombing assault of power, endurance, and technique, coursing its way along the right side of the gully. Easily the wall's longest and hardest route, it links *Repeat Offender* into *Villain* at the crux panel. Likely the most difficult pitch at Smith.

❹ Villain 5.14a ★★★
A gorgeous line with an ugly history (see next page). A steep start and a few bolts of 5.13b lead to the infamous crux on the brownish red panel peppered with shallow pockets. Basically 5.12 climbing surrounding a grievous boulder problem. Stick clip the 2nd bolt.

❺ Lucky Pigeon 5.13c ★★★
A good link-up. Starts up *White Wedding*, skipping to the right, before the rest jug in the mini-roof and power crux of *White Wedding*, into the pumper finish of *Villain*.

❻ White Wedding 5.13d ★★★★
Two distinct cruxes define this popular testpiece. The first battles through micro-knobs at the 5th and 6th bolts right before a strenuous "rest" in the overlap. The second crux comes higher above the 7th bolt, where an insecure series of slaps and grabs force you to forgo clipping the 8th bolt. Get through both cruxes and all you have to do is battle the pump up the final mid-range 5.12 roof and headwall.

❼ Bad Man 5.14a ★★★★
A power endurance dream, or nightmare, depending on your fitness. There's no good shake before the 8th bolt, below which lie two cruxes: a streno undercling problem at the 4th bolt and a powerful, reachy sequence at the 7th. Between the two cruxes the climbing is continuously difficult and never allows you to recover. Sketch through to the 8th bolt and you still have to make it through the 12c headwall that guards the anchor.

❽ Aggro Monkey 5.13b ★★★★
The original route on the wall. This pumpy line is arguably the best 13b at Smith. The business kicks in immediately with a cryptic section of awkward climbing under the roof. (After clipping the second bolt, reach back and unclip the first to eliminate rope drag.) After bleeding out in a knee bar, pull the crux moves (powerful and crimpy) over the roof to a massive jug. The rest of the climbing is not as severe, but not by much, requiring strong lock-offs on sustained pockets and edges between good holds. **Warning:** there are

AGGRO GULLY

two dogging bolts on the route (the 7th and 9th bolts), which are nothing more than glorified plant hangers—screw-in eyebolts from the hardware store. Seriously. They'll hold body weight but likely little else. You have been warned...

9 Mama Docus 5.13c ★★
A significant step up from *Aggro Monkey* that shares the same roof start but dodges right. The crux is getting to, around, and off, the "basketball", an evil sloping knob. There is also a direct start that has yet to see an ascent—likely due to the finger-torturing mono-to-a-mono-to-a-mono sequence.

10 Scene of the Crime 5.13b ★★★
Another route with two distinct cruxes. The first is right off the deck on small pockets, and the second takes on a mean mono move higher up. Tall climbers can finish direct, while everyone sub-six-foot will dart left at the last bolt to avoid a massive reach.

11 Crime Wave 5.13c ★
A direct start to *Scene of the Crime* that ascends rotten rock and uses a bolt-on flake. Extremely unpopular.

12 The Quickening 5.12c ★★★★
The warm-up for the harder routes in the gully. Starts off with steep pulls through a roof on two drilled/enhanced pockets to a moderate hanging-slab rest. Above the rest is the crux: surf out to a left-hand crimper, high-step right foot in a drilled pocket, and

make a long reach right-handed to a big pocket. Short people might find this crux nearly impossible. Sustained climbing for two more bolts and then a bolt of cruiser 5.10 to the anchors.

13 Disposable Heroes 5.13c ★★
(aka Disposable Handholds)
The most heavily glued route at Smith (by a mile), this route would be dust on the ground if not for all the epoxy. After punching through the opening roof of *The Quickening*, cut left and follow the glue-smeared offset corner. Crux at two-thirds height. Actually quite popular and climbs very well considering its appearance.

The following two routes are on the east-facing side of gully. These pitches are not shown in the photos but are easily identified by the chalk. There are a few other routes on this wall but they're junk.

14 Toxic 5.11b ★★★★
Looming over the abyss on the far left, this juggy climb is a Smith classic. The dyno or deadpoint at the third bolt makes for spectacular photos.

15 Up For Grabs 5.11d ★★★★
About 100 ft uphill from *Toxic* is this line up a slab and into a bulge. The first five bolts angle up to the left (a 5.12a goes straight up and shares the same start). A tricky series of technical moves are required to get through the bulge. Above the bulge there are two options: a dyno (straight up) or skirting left on pockets and crimps.

Tim Garland on *Slit Your Wrist* 5.13b (page 26).

2
COCAINE GULLY

It's not hard to imagine the Cocaine Wall as a onetime chic warm-up zone (circa 1988) for anorexic sportos to amp up for the day by snorting back lines of low-grade Charlie and cranking Ministry on the jam box. Sadly Cocaine Gully's heyday seems to have long since passed (where have all the good days gone?). Visitors today, however, drinking their chai tea and humming Jack Johnson songs, will still find a tasty stash of 5.10 to 5.11+ knob-job classics to get their fix on at the vertical Cocaine Wall (including the must-do *Vomit Launch* 5.11b). At the base of the Cocaine Gully is the Western Ship's river face, which hosts a handful of striking 5.13 and up technical pocket routes as well as some popular bolted slab moderates and a curiously unpopular 5.9 multi-pitch trad line. Cocaine Wall gets shade until after-noon, while the river face sector is hot, hot, hot, soaking up the sun until very late in the day.

Dividing the two sectors is a nasty-ass jumble of mas-sive boulders, through which you must scramble in order to reach the Cocaine Wall. There are two ways to access the Cocaine Wall—neither of which is pleasant. Option A is third-class scrambling up a claustrophobic "Nostril" (aka The Haunta Virus Hole) on the right side through pigeon shit and lung-choking dust. Yummy. Take a deep breath and punch it for the blue sky. Option B is on the left side. It's less vile but involves exposed fourth-class moves in which the crux is not putting your hand in the ever-present rat/pi-geon/bat piss that varnishes the rock. Seriously, it's nasty. If you want to kill your dog, bring it this way. Better yet, keep the dog and anyone without climbing savvy far away from these loose and dirty approaches.

NB: If you, your rope, your belayer, your pack, or some-one next to you happens to knock a rock loose from the Cocaine Wall ledge, yell "Rock!" If someone is crawling up the Nostril, the rock will brain'em for sure.

13 mins

21 routes

5.6- 5.7 5.8 5.9 5.10 5.11 5.12 5.13 5.14

sun p.m.

sun all day

DON'T MISS	
Slit Your Wrist 5.13b	☐
Crack Babies 5.12b	☐
Bloodshot 5.11c	☐
Vomit Launch 5.11b	☐

WESTERN SHIP, RIVER FACE

Nostril access to Cocaine Wall

❹ Phone Call From Satan 5.9 ★★ ☐
Another popular moderate slab. The access pitch to *Power*.

❺ Caffeine Free 5.10a ★★ ☐
The sister route just to the left of the above 5.9, though not as good or as popular.

❻ Time's Up 5.13a/b ★★★ ☐
This rig ain't for techno-phobes. Demanding delicate footwork and precision edge crimping, the upper part will spank the grunting gym monkeys. A 12b start yields to a camper sit-down ledge, allowing climbers to fully de-pump before tackling the headwall.

❼ Mr. Yuck 5.14a ★★★ ☐
Climbs the crux of *Slit Your Wrist* to a rest, then busts right up to the *Time's Up* anchors. Some think *Slit Your Wrist* is the crux.

❽ Slit Your Wrist 5.13b ★★★★ ☐
A technical overhanging arête. Beta intensive. Follows the same starting sequence as *Time's Up*, but branches left and finishes on *The Blade*.

❾ The Blade 5.12a ★★★ ☐
The top section of *Slit Your Wrist*. Accessed from atop a giant boulder at the far right side of the Cocaine Wall. Unfortunately the crux comes right off the belay so unless you're psyched on soloing technical 5.12 arete slaps with 50 feet of air beneath you, you'll need to stick clip the first bolt.

❿ Chicken McNuggets 5.10b ★★★ ☐
Top quality knobs; some impossibly solid. Trust 'em — they're bomber. The crux is at the first bolt. Work the crack with your left, and pimp small knobs with your right. Once you hit the first big knob and clip the second bolt it's cruiser.

❶ Power 5.13b ★★ ☐
A steep pitch on the upper wall that packs a solid pump and has one very hard move. The hanging belay at the base of the pitch is commonly reached via a bolted 5.9 slab or via the first pitch of *Solar*.

"Is Vomit Launch the best 11b in the Park? You be the judge."

❷ Solar 5.9R ★★ ☐
Bring on the masses! This three-pitch trad line offers a fine alternative to the bolted slabs below. The first pitch starts from the base of *Toxic*. Rappel with double ropes. Small to medium gear.
1. 5.8 Sketch around the corner from *Toxic* to the hanging belay at the base of *Power*.
2. 5.9 Cruise up a crack to a comfy belay ledge. Short pitch. Possible to combine with Pitch 1 but not recommended due to rope drag.
3. 5.9 Follow the corner to the ridge crest. Rappel from here or for full kook points, scramble up the 4th class ridge to the summit.

❸ The Purple Headed Warrior 5.7 ★★ ☐
A fun moderate slab on the far right side of the river face.

⓫ Cocaine Crack 5.11b ★★ ☐
The rock looks like shit, but it climbs really well. Honest. No stopper moves. Small to medium gear.

⓬ Vomit Launch 5.11b ★★★★ ☐
The best 11b in the park? You be the judge. A little sporty to the first bolt, you may want a stick clip. A reachy, thin crux move to a huge hole at the 5th bolt is the hardest move, but the true crux is fighting off the burly pump to the anchors.

⓭ Freebase 5.12a ★★★ ☐
Very sustained pebbling and edging. Tenuous clips. Get suckered into going the wrong way up high (*Hmmm ... do you go left or right? Sorry, I don't remember...*) and you'll whip for sure.

COCAINE WALL

⑭ Powder Up the Nose 5.10d ★★ ☐
Follows the water streak. Some seriously small pebbles for feet. Technical and sustained. A tough pitch for the grade.

⑮ Shake 'N Flake 5.11b ★ ☐
The name should be reversed—first comes the flake, then at the stout second bolt crux, comes the shake.

⑯ Rabid 5.12b ★ ☐
Thin and cruxy through the first two bolts. Easier up high.

⑰ Bound In Bogota 5.11a ★★ ☐
Hard down low then fun knobs and pockets to the chains.

⑱ Deep Impact 5.10c ★★ ☐
This route is left of *Bound In Bogota* (#17) and not shown in the photo above.

⑲ Armageddon 5.11a ★★ ☐
This route is left of *Deep Impact*.

The next two routes described are a short way up the hill on the opposite side of Cocaine Gully and are not shown in the photograph above.

⑳ Bloodshot 5.11c ★★★ ☐
The obvious long climb with many bolts (about 50 feet downhill from *Crack Babies* #21). A varied, pumpy route.

㉑ Crack Babies 5.12b ★★★ ☐
Gym-climbers rejoice: The next route uphill (right) from Bloodshot is atypically steep and thuggish for Smith. Climbs a steep gray depression on big holds.

3

MORNING GLORY WALL

10 mins

35 routes

5.6- 5.7 5.8 5.9 5.10 5.11 5.12 5.13 5.14

sun all day

DON'T MISS	
Vicious Fish 5.13c/d	☐
Churning In the Wake 5.13a	☐
Kings of Rap 5.12d	☐
Overboard 5.11b	☐
Lion's Chair 5.11a	☐
Magic Light 5.11a	☐
Zebra/Zion 5.10a	☐
Nine Gallon Buckets 5.9	☐
Five Gallon Buckets 5.8	☐

Facing dead south, the Morning Glory Wall area is a sun trap, making it the place to be on cold, sunny winter days but a bolt-melting furnace in the warmer months. Whether you're a visiting Euro star or wet-wooler PNW newbie, there are enough quality pitches here to keep you busy for days. The three main sectors, Churning Buttress, Overboard Area, and Zion Area, are stacked with everything from beginner slabs to 5.13 projects to mega-classic multi-pitchers. Expect people—lots of them. The Morning Glory Wall area is the prime warm-up spot for nearly everyone since it's one of the first frontside areas reached and has a bathroom conveniently a stone's throw away for the mid-morning post-coffee poo. Climbers anxiously lining up for both the routes and the bathroom is a common weekend sight.

Ellen Powick
High above I-15 on *Horse Latitudes*, VRG, Arizona.

 KOLIN POWICK

Black Diamond™

BlackDiamondEquipment.com
801.278.5533

CHURNING BUTTRESS

Housing the best concentration of south-facing 5.12 and 5.13 sport routes at Smith, this wall of stellar stone is the place to see and be seen on winter days. Expect crowds, fixed draws, and an endless procession of locals hiking the piss out of the routes (especially *Churning in the Wake*). On the plus side you'll never get stumped figuring out the moves on any of the routes—the locals have them wired to death and can give you move-by-move beta.

❶ Oxygen 5.13a/b ★★★ ☐
The sustained crux of technical sidepulls with bad feet comes around the 2nd and 3rd bolts. Tall climbers can lean off the *Da Kine* boulder to pre-clip the first bolt, while shorties will need to stick clip it or face nasty ground-fall potential. A cerebral test certain to bout gym climbers.

❷ Jam Master Jay 5.13d ★★ ☐
A grievous 15 foot direct start to *Oxygen*. One of the most bouldery sections of climbing at Smith. A grim, powerful V-double-digit sequence on micro knobs and underclings, leads directly into the crux of *Oxygen*. It wouldn't be outrageous to one day see boulderers blanketing the base with crashpads and tackling this direct start as a boulder problem in itself.

❸ Da Kine Corner 5.12c ★★★ ☐
Another must-stick-clip-first-bolt route. Desperate moves near the first bolt access sustained climbing on impeccable red stone.

❹ White Heat 5.14? ★ ☐
Unrepeated since the 5.13c/d first ascent by Alan Watts (who else?) in 1988. The crux mono pocket busted at the second to last bolt. Has seen many attempts with no one bagging the second ascent. Basically 5.12+ climbing to a grievous one-move sequence on the broken pocket.

❺ Kings of Rap 5.12d ★★★★ ☐
Harder moves than *Churning in the Wake*, but with better rests. Tough getting through the slab and into the roof. A sustained headwall (pumpy!) of bullet stone guards the anchors. Typically has fixed slings on the bolts below the roof to reduce rope drag.

❻ Waste Case 5.13b ★★★ ☐
A direct start into *Kings of Rap* that cuts left at the roof to finish up *Vicious Fish's* incredible arête. Bouldery start and cruxy pulling the roof. Called "the best 13 in the park" by one-time Smith master Jim Karn.

❼ Vicious Fish 5.13c/d ★★★★ ☐
Locals often talk of needing "good fishing conditions" to redpoint this desperate line. Very hard at the fourth bolt. At the 6th bolt is the "fishing move" where you need to slap, slap, and slap right-handed. Shares the rest jug on *Churning* and then busts right up the amazing arête.

❽ Churning in the Wake 5.13a ★★★★ ☐
The Smith Rock classic 13a. A super popular warm-up, project, or warm-down, depending on your fitness and local status. Basically 12a to the 4th bolt, 12b to the 5th, 12c to the 6th, 12d to the 7th, and 13a to the chains. The final move to the anchor jug used to be the scene of go-for-broke lunges off a three-finger pocket. The pocket has since busted, requiring a more in-control punch to the jug off a marginal pinch aka the "man hold."

❾ Churning Sky 5.13a ★★★★ ☐
An extension of *Churning in the Wake* that doesn't bump the grade (thanks to some good rests), but does make for a super proud full pitch on five-star stone finishing on *Vicious Fish's* anchor. The upper 5.12-ish crux move is quite reachy, forcing short climbers to use micro holds where full-sized adults can do a huge span.

❿ Churning in the Ozone 5.13b ★★★★ ☐
After the *Churning Sky* crux, snake left for more mid-range 5.12 climbing on pockets and edges. A touch reachy for midgets, gnomes, trolls, and anyone else who's sub 5'9". An incredible pitch requiring a 60-meter rope to lower.

⓫ Taco Chips 5.13a ★★★ ☐
Holds have broken over time, bumping the original grade up a notch to 13a. Tough moves sandwiched around a good rest halfway. Thin and technical down low, especially around the 4th bolt. Precision footwork a must.

⓬ Doritos 5.12c ★★ ☐
Combines the best climbing on *Cool Ranch Flavor* (bottom half) and *Taco Chips* (upper half). Traverse off of CRF into the *Taco Chips* rest jug and then gun for the anchors.

⓭ Nacho Cheese 5.12c ★ ☐
Combines the worst climbing on *Taco Chips* (bottom half) and *Cool Ranch Flavor* (upper half). Traverse off of *Taco Chips* at the rest jug and then gun for the anchors. An Ian Caldwell link-up special unlikely (for obvious reasons) to have seen a second ascent.

⓮ Cool Ranch Flavor 5.11a ★★ ☐
Cruiser buckets lead to a move out right and a cruxy sequence. The hardest moves can be avoided by continuing up the chossy crack and then angling toward the anchors.

OVERBOARD AREA

A very popular area, especially for warming-up on 5.11s before proj-ing at the Churning Buttress. Long and pumpy is the gig here as most of the routes have extensions, some requiring a 70-meter rope and/or rappels.

1 Nine Gallon Buckets 5.9/5.10c ★★★★ ☐
Fun 5.9 huecos to the first set of anchors with the hardest bit getting off the ground. A strenuous 5.10 undercling and sidepull sequence above the anchors leads to another set of anchors (skip'em) and into the best 5.8 honeycomb pockets in the park. You need a 60-meter rope to lower from the top anchors.

2 Overboard 5.11b/5.11c+ ★★★★ ☐
(aka Overly Bored)
The second most popular 5.11 at Smith. Don't be surprised on this and the following route if someone starts up after and unclips your first 3 bolts. Locals have this climb brutally wired—thus the debasing nickname. Basically 5.9 climbing to a V2 sidepull/barndoor crux with crappy feet to 5.9 climbing. If you have a 70-meter rope, skip the first set of anchors and continue up via excellent and airy 5.10+ edges to a recently installed anchor at 35-meters for a full-voyage pitch (aka *Fully Bored*). The grade is still 5.11c but just barely. Above the new anchor is an additional bolt's worth of crappy climbing to the old anchors, but then you'll need to rap off with two ropes—which isn't worth the hassle.

3 Magic Light 5.11a/5.12b/5.12b ★★★★ ☐
(aka Tragic Flight)
The most popular 5.11 at Smith. Excellent climbing on mostly big holds. Shares the first three bolts of *Overboard* and then moves left (thin and cruxy) with continuous moves to the first set of anchors at 70 feet (5.11a). Like *Overboard*, this route has a rope-stretching extension, once neglected because the anchors were too high to lower off with a single 70-meter cord. Now however, an anchor has been added at 35-meters, which allows you to tack on five bolts worth of outstanding 12b climbing (cruxy right off the first set of anchors) and lower off with a 70-meter rope. The original extension keeps going even further up a scrappy, scabby slab (12b) and is super *not* recommended. This complete extension has been dubbed *Tragic Flight* after Tim Garland was lowered off the end of his rope while trying to return to the first set of anchors. Mr. Garland amazingly survived his 70-foot freefall, and was LifeFlight'ed from Smith with multiple injuries including two shattered heels and a busted back. Tim recovered and is now a caberet dancer!

4 Energy Crisis 5.12b ★★ ☐
A thin start keeps most people from leading this edgy route. Almost everyone does it by lowering down from the *Magic Light* anchors and top-roping from the second bolt on up for a fun 11a pump.

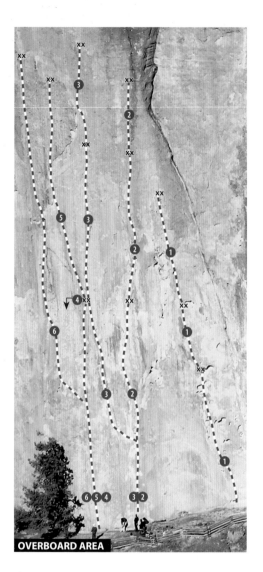

OVERBOARD AREA

5 Sketch Pad 5.12d ★★ ☐
About as overlooked as a route can get, this extension to *Energy Crisis* rarely, if ever, has chalk on it. This is mostly due to the route's too high anchors, requiring a double-rope rappel to get off. Can also be linked with the first 70 feet of *Magic Light*. If this extension were to ever get an anchor retro'd at 35-meters, it would get four stars and rocket into popularity.

6 Mane Line 5.13a ★ ☐
If you know someone who has climbed this line, get their autograph as they are one of maybe three people who have done so. Start with *Energy Crisis* and then snake left to jumbo buckets, shake out, and then wander up the sustained-looking 5.12 headwall. Also requires a double-rope rappel to descend.

ZION AREA

A stacked wall with high-quality lines from 5.9 to 5.11 on fun buckets and thin faces. Also home to two mega multi-pitch trad lines. It's not uncommon to see ropes on *all* of the bolted lines.

ZEBRA/ZION

❶ Lion's Chair 5.11a ★★★★ ☐

The obvious dihedral directly in front of the approach trail. One hundred feet of thin stemming and tricky jamming. The crux can be avoided (aka *The Mayor Of Sissyville* variant) by stepping right into the potholes. Skip the first set of anchors (aka *The Mayor Of Sissyville* anchors) and punch it through a few more pumpy moves to reach a cruiser 5.8 jam crack (a popular roost for pigeons) and the second bolted anchor. Four pitches long, but no one has done more than the first pitch in years because the upper climbing is less-than-spectacular and requires a walk-off down Cocaine Gully. Small to medium gear.

❷ Dandy Line 5.12d ★ ☐

In the center of the section of wall that is corralled by a fence is this lonely route that no one does. The streno-looking nature of the initial seam moves keeps most people from even considering booting up.

❸ Zebra Seam 5.11d ★★★ ☐

The bolts take the sting out this one-time trad shake-fest but the climbing is still technical and demanding.

❹ Zebra Direct 5.11a ★ ☐

Thin and technical face moves to easy buckets.

❺ Zebra/Zion 5.10b ★★★★ ☐

A must-do line rocketing up the 350-foot wall. One of the best 5.10s in the park with an incredible final pitch that you'll be gushing about for months afterward. Combines the first two pitches of *Zebra* and then steps right (to avoid *Zebra's* final two pitches of junk) and up to the impressive headwall of *Zion*. Easily identified by the stunning right-facing dihedral 100 feet up. Mostly medium to hand-sized gear needed. Trivia note: Fred Beckey climbed this pitch at the age of 78.

1. 5.10a Traverse across the huge huecos (5.8) using long slings to avoid rope drag or do *Zebra Direct* (5.11d) for full value. Skip the hanging belay (*Zebra Direct's* anchors) and continue upwards through the 5.10 crux layaway moves and into the perfect dihedral to an awesome ledge with bolted anchors. A long pitch, roughly 180 feet.

2. 5.8 Continue up the crack but after 30 feet step right (otherwise the crack leads you to the *Choss In America* ledge and a final pitch of 4th-class gully crap) and make an exposed, unprotected traverse on knobs, rising upwards on a sparsely protected slab crack to the base of the headwall.

3. 5.9 Don't let your partner lead this pitch. It's mega. Give'em whatever they want, promise'em what ever they desire—just make sure you get this lead. It's the best 5.9 pitch at Smith. Traverse up and out the flake on hand-swallowing jugs. The sinker holds make for idiot-proof protection—just drop in any medium-sized nut and it'll be bombproof. Radical exposure that'll have you laughing. After the flake, traverse left 10 feet on a large ledge and climb a water chute to anchors. Descend via the Cocaine Gully.

❻ Lion Zion 5.10c ★★★ ☐

The bolted line to the right of the *Zion's* dihedral. Starts off the *Zebra Direct* anchors and plumblines up positive grips to the anchors down and right of *Zion's* big ledge. Not much chalk on this line so be prepared for some delicate routefinding. Cool route that deserves more traffic.

❼ Choss in America 5.12c ★★★ ☐

Well off the beaten track far below, this gorgeous face sees little to no action. Too bad. It's a sweet pitch with outrageous exposure. From the *Zion* ledge continue up a 5.8 crack to a massive ledge. From here crimp your way through multiple 5.12 cruxes on edges and pockets. Walk off down Cocaine Gully.

❽ Gumby 5.10b ★★★ ☐

Get through the balancy start crux section and you'll surely coast the 5.6 buckets to the *Zebra Direct* anchor. Hard moves for the grade.

❾ Morning Sky 5.10c ★★★ ☐

An excellent and demanding continuation of *Gumby*, heading up more technical climbing rather than cutting right to *Zebra Direct's* anchors.

ZION BASE

⑩ Cat Scan 5.11b ★★★ ☐
If *Morning Sky* isn't enough, keep going! *Cat Scan* is the ultra-rare extension-to-an-extension usually reserved for Seattle's Little Si or Rifle. Shake out at *Morning Sky's* anchors and punch it through a couple of crux sections (one near the anchor, one half way up) to *Zion's* ledge. Rap with two ropes or keep going up *Zebra/Zion*. An excellent, super long sport pitch of edges and pockets.

⑪ Light on the Path 5.10a ★★★ ☐
Buckets galore on this fun romp. No hard moves just jug after jug after jug. Can also be used as a start to *Cat Scan*—creating the even more ultra-rare link-up into an extension of an extension.

⑫ The Outsiders 5.9 ★★★ ☐
Same deal as *Light on the Path*—buckets and buckets.

⑬ Five Gallon Buckets 5.8 ★★★★ ☐
If you ever see someone not on this mega-hyper popular route you are either there in the middle of the night or hallucinating. An easier version of the two previous

routes, this line is likely the most popular 5.8 in the park. Not a good lead for the beginner though, as the bolts are a bit more spaced than your average gym route.

⑭ Lion's Jaw 5.8 ★★★ ☐
Located 50 feet to the left of *Five Gallon Buckets*, this popular moderate corner is the scene of gear-pulling and ankle-breaking groundfalls. The start is not too bad but high traffic has polished the stone to near zero-friction and the gear requires savvy placements. Difficulties ease above mid-height. The climb does continue above the bolted belay, but it's total trash and no one has likely done the upper section of 5.7 junk in 20 years. Mostly small to medium gear.

⑮ Tammy Baker's Face 5.10c ★★ ☐
Not quite as bad as Preacher Jim's old wife's nasty mug, but it's no Selma Hayek either. Rap with two ropes.
1. 5.9 Move up the face picking away at Tammy's pimples and knobs to a comfy ledge with a bolted belay.
2. 5.10c A great pitch, highlighted by an airy pull over a bulge.

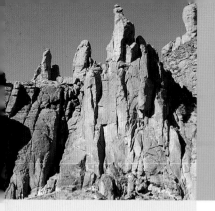

4 Peanut
4TH Horseman
Cinnamon Slab

🚶 12 mins

16 routes

5.6- 5.7 5.8 5.9 5.10 5.11 5.12 5.13 5.14

| sun all day |
| sun a.m. |

DON'T MISS	
Headless Horseman 5.10d	☐
Pack Animal Direct 5.10b	☐
Cry Baby 5.9	☐
Cinnamon Slab 5.6	☐

Tucked between the Dihedrals and the Zion Wall is this trio of sectors loaded with fun 5.5 to 5.11 climbs. The Fourth Horseman's cracks are curiously underappreciated, while the Cinnamon Slab is as popular as any place at Smith. A spattering of moderate sport climbs on the Peanut will feed those with a bolt-clipping jones.

This area, like almost every cliff on the frontside, bakes in the sun so don't plan on spending a June mid-day here unless you want to fry yourself extra crispy. Cinnamon Slab falls in the shade by mid-afternoon, but the Fourth Horseman cooks in the solar oven nearly all day.

Brooke Sandahl soloing *Cinnamon Slab* 5.6 (page 40).

THE PEANUT

Just left of the Zion Wall is this fun 65-foot block with four routes. A great option for bolted moderates if the Zion Wall is packed.

1 Popism 5.11b ★★ ☐
A funky arête climb that has been retro-bolted to make the climb safer to lead.

2 Pop Goes the Nubbin 5.10a ★★★ ☐
A nice introduction to Smith Rock knob tugging.

3 Peanut Brittle 5.8 ★★ ☐
A similar but easier version of *Pop Goes the Nubbin*.

4 Hop On Pop 5.8 ★★★ ☐
A cruxy start leads to an easy slab. A good novice lead.

4TH HORSEMAN

A great collection of 5.11-and-under cracks, many better than the nearby and super popular *Karate Crack*. All the pitches are steep and clean with good protection.

1 Snuffy Smith 5.9 ★★ ☐
The next route to the left of the Peanut. Up the face, over to a crack, and then some arête moves. A fun, varied, and safe lead.

2 Tuff It Out 5.10a ★★ ☐
Nothing special about this line to the left of *Snuffy Smith* (except for the unique honeycomb buckets to start), but if you need to get in just one more pitch before heading back to car ... well sure, why not?

3 Name Unknown 5.10d ★★ ☐
A long pitch if you skip the intermediate belay. You'll need a 70-meter rope to lower from the upper anchors though. Tricky bulge at the first bolt (you can avoid this by traversing in from the right) to a cool roof section. (Up to the first anchor the climbing is mid-range 5.10 and makes for a fine route in itself.) Above the first anchors, continue up easy ground and then step back onto the face proper for more exciting edge climbing.

4 Friday's Jinx 5.7 ★★★ ☐
A mellow two-pitch trad jaunt up on the first crack to the left of the above route.
1. 5.7 From the high ground head up a few steep moves (to the left of the choss) and then move right to the corner and into the main line proper. Belay at a big block. Give this lead to your partner as the next one is the Money Pitch.
2. 5.7 A fantastic pitch up the big left facing corner.

5 Crack of Infinity 5.10b ★★★ ☐
A spectacular trad line with an outstanding second pitch. Two single rope raps will get you down. Small and hand-sized gear needed.
1. 5.10b Crux through the steep crack (easier than it looks, don't worry) then traverse over to the *Friday's Jinx* belay. You can also do the crack just to the right (10a) for a touch easier start but it's not nearly as good.
2. 5.9 Sweet hands through the headwall splitting flake. You can belay at the ledge (how it was done originally), but it's better to continue up the overhanging 5.9 handcrack for 20 more feet to the bolted rap anchors.

6 Calamity Jam 5.10c ★★★ ☐
A fantastic crack pitch that shouldn't be missed. Much better than other nearby, more popular pitches such as *Karate Crack*. Crux through the undercling jams down low and then plug into the high-quality finger crack. Small and medium gear needed.

7 Catastrophic Crack 5.12a ★★ ☐
Short and testy direct start to *Calamity Jam*. Thin gear safely protects the moves but most people just toprope it from the *Calamity Jam* anchors.

8 Sandbag 5.10c ★★ ☐
Another variant semi-direct start to *Calamity Jam*. Not nearly as good as the regular start. Often toproped. Small and medium gear needed.

9 Name Unknown 5.11c ★★ ☐
A little sport action for those tiring of all of the Fourth Horseman's cracks. Starts just to the right of the large dihedral. Difficulties ease the higher you get.

10 Pack Animal Direct 5.10b ★★★★ ☐
A mega classic corner with cool stemming and jams. Short and sweet with excellent nut protection where it's hard. A must do. Small to medium gear needed. From the anchor you can rap or continue up *Pack Animal* or *Sundancer* to the right.

11 Name Unknown 5.10c ★★ ☐
A clip-up on the arête just left of *Pack Animal Direct*. Hard near the third bolt. Can be linked with *Headless Horseman* for a super long sport pitch (which then requires a 70-meter rope).

12 Pack Animal 5.8 ★★★ ☐
A great moderate trad excursion, requiring small to hand-sized gear.
1. 5.8 Up the easy crack and then step 20-feet to the right and up the crack/corner/face. The traverse is intimidating as the climb is runout to a pin. Not that great, so if you're up for it, do the direct start.
2. 5.8 Ascend the beautiful left-facing corner to an awkwardly low two-bolt anchor.

THE PEANUT AND 4TH HORSEMAN

⑬ **Sundancer** 5.10b ★

You can skip the final pitch of *Pack Animal* and climb this so-so face. Nothing special. Bring small to medium gear to protect the climbing before the first bolt.

⑭ **Equus** 5.11b ★★

A bolted final pitch to the summit of the *Fourth Horseman*. Reached from the top of *Pack Animal* or *Sundancer*. Walk off to Cinnamon Slab rappels (next page). There are routes that summit the other three Horsemen, but all are crumbly and loose. If you just gotta get some summits in, however, they make for easy ticks after completing *Equus*.

⑮ **Headless Horseman** 5.10d ★★★★

A stellar somewhat-technical sport pitch on the far left side. Solo up the easy crack (shared with *Pack Animal*) and then launch onto the face. Crux comes near the fourth and fifth bolts. It's a long and involved pitch with outstanding position, and you'll need a 70-meter cord to lower all the way to the ground from the anchor. Alternatively you can lower to the slab atop the easy crack, untie, and scramble down to the west.

⑯ **Equine-imity** 5.10b ★★

Juts left above the easy crack start of *Headless Horseman*. Cruxy at the second bulge.

CINNAMON SLAB

The busy scene here is often a rescue situation waiting to happen. Be extremely careful during the crowded weekends when seemingly every Day One beginner in the Pacific Northwest is on, below, or near the cliff—shit is constantly being knocked down from above (including gear, ropes, helmets, and nut tools) by thumby novices. Those caveats aside, the Cinnamon Slab is an excellent spot for newcomers to the sport—as long as you are careful! The climbs are low-angle, amply bolted, and have good ledges at the anchors, making for safe leads.

Two single-rope raps from the top of Cinnamon Slab will get you back down to terra firma. **NB: Try not to rap off the anchors of Karate Crack, thereby making them useless to climbers on the Karate Wall.** If Cinnamon Slab is busy, stay out of people's way by walking over to the anchors on *Rodney's Chocolate Frosted Love Donut* to rap. Also note that scree and talus is everywhere on top of Cinnamon Slab so be extremely careful when rigging the raps otherwise you could end up drilling someone below in the head.

CINNAMON SLAB

❶ Lichen It 5.8 ★★★ ☐
The furthest right of the Cinnamon Slab routes. After the initial crux section the climbing eases to cruiser 5.6. Super popular.

❷ Right Slab Crack 5.5 ★★ ☐
Only done because you can easily toprope it from the *Lichen It* or *Easy Reader* anchors. If you want to lead the line, bring medium to hand-sized gear. Somewhat super-popular.

❸ Easy Reader 5.6 ★★★ ☐
Similar to *Lichen It*, the crux is the first couple of bolts. Super-duper-popular.

❹ Left Slab Crack 5.4 ★ ☐
Similar to *Right Slab Crack* only it's on the left and not as good. Most people toprope this crack from *Night Flight*. Bring medium to hand-sized gear. Somewhat-not-so popular.

❺ Night Flight 5.5 ★★★ ☐
First-time leaders line here! Bolted for the masses, this line is a common devirginizing lead. Super-popular.

❻ Ginger Snap 5.8 ★★★ ☐
A face-climbing alternative to the first pitch of *Cinnamon Slab* (can also be TR'd from that route's anchors). Cool climbing on excellent rock. Super-duper popular.

❼ Cinnamon Slab 5.6 ★★★★ ☐
Few routes get as much traffic as this two-pitch crack line. It has everything for the newbie! Multi-pitching, gear placements, a comfy belay ledge with two sets of anchors, and clean stone. Get here early for this classic line, and bring medium to hand-sized gear. Descend via two single-rope rappels. Super-double-duper popular.
1. 5.6 Easy jamming on the rampy corner gets tougher up high where the crack widens to big hands. Luckily there are some good face knobs on the right to bail you out. Belay on the broad ledge from either of the two bolted anchors.
2. 5.5 A few awkward face moves to get around the wide crack then sail up the easy corner to the bolted rap anchors.

❽ Cinnamon Toast 5.7 ☐
A rarely done variation to the classic second pitch of *Cinnamon Slab*. Step left onto the face after 15 feet. Bring some gear to compliment the two rusty bolts.

❾ Cry Baby 5.9 ★★★★ ☐
A much better option than the *Cinnamon Toast* variant to the 2nd pitch of *Cinnamon Slab*. After skirting the wide crack above the bolt step left and soak up the airy position following the shiny bolts. Classic exposure.

❿ Rodney's Chocolate Frosted Love Donut 5.9 ☐
Hey, how about one more variation to *Cinnamon Slab's* second pitch! Another waste-of-time bolted line, this time heading up and right from the ledge.

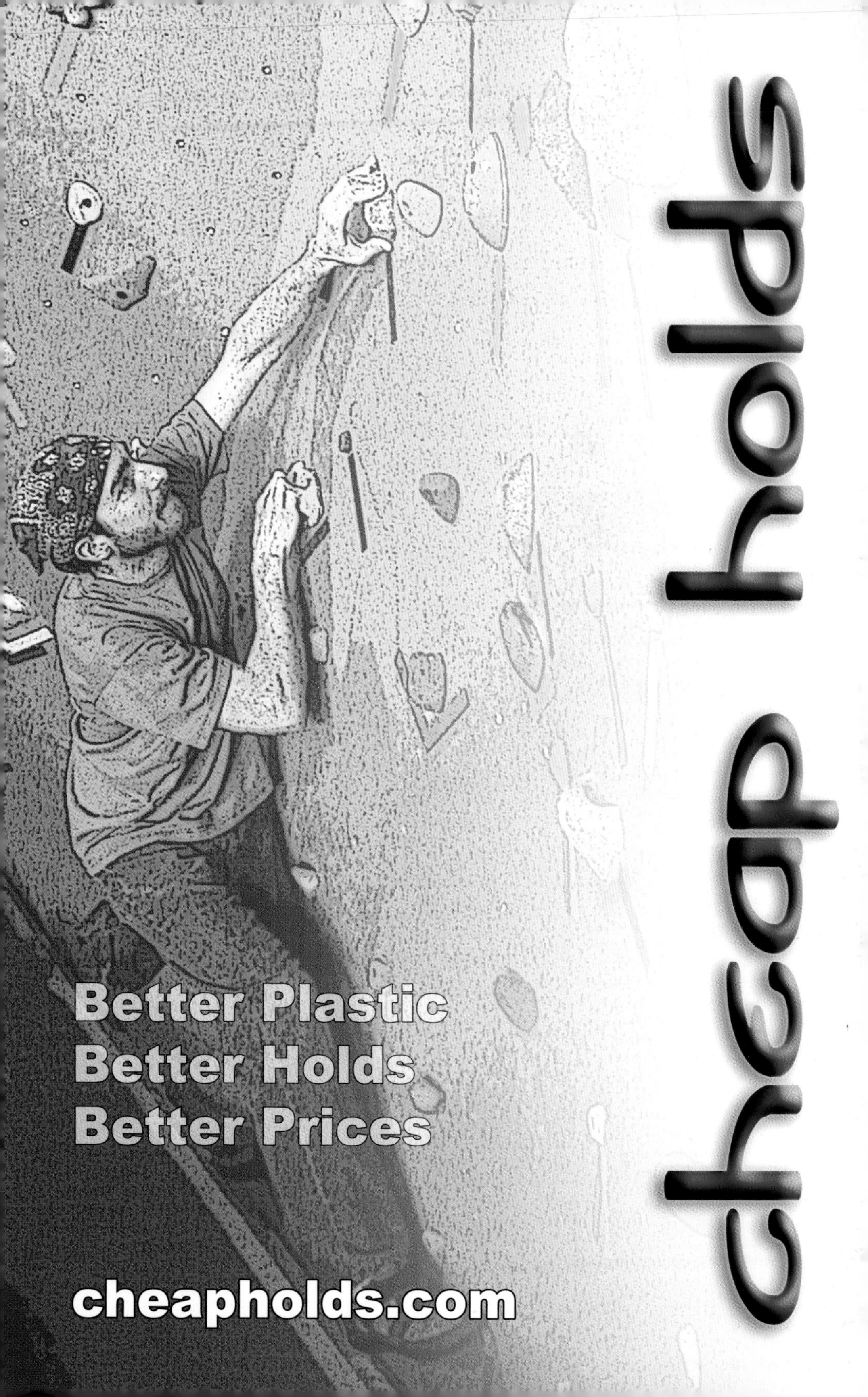

cheap holds

**Better Plastic
Better Holds
Better Prices**

cheapholds.com

5
THE DIHEDRALS

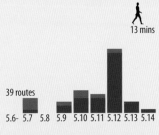

13 mins

39 routes

5.6- 5.7 5.8 5.9 5.10 5.11 5.12 5.13 5.14

sun all day

sun a.m.

DON'T MISS	
To Bolt or Not To Be 5.14a	☐
Darkness At Noon 5.13a	☐
Karate Wall 5.12c	☐
Last Waltz 5.12c	☐
Chain Reaction 5.12c	☐
Go Dog Go 5.12c	☐
Crossfire 5.12b	☐
Firing Line 5.12b	☐
Latest Rage 5.12b	☐
Vision 5.12b	☐
Power Dive 5.12a	☐
Take A Powder 5.12a	☐
Heinous Cling 5.12a	☐
Sunshine Dihedral 5.11d	☐
Karate Crack 5.10a	☐
Moonshine Dihedral 5.9	☐
Bookworm 5.7	☐
Bunny Face 5.7	☐

This is where Smith Rock's sport climbing history was made. The iconic Dihedrals are an impressive accordion of dead vertical walls and arêtes that have drawn climbers from around the world. The Dihedrals are a living museum of benchmark routes, including Smith's first rap-bolted climb *Watts Tots*, first 5.13 *Darkness At Noon*, America's first 5.14a *To Bolt Or Not To Be*, as well as mega-popular, must-do 5.12s such as *Heinous Cling, Karate Wall, Latest Rage, Last Waltz, Chain Reaction,* and *Sunshine Dihedral.*

Everyone who comes to Smith will climb at the Dihedrals. The dirt at the base has been pounded down to concrete and the climbs are so heavily chalked you can spot the holds from the parking lot. Numerous trail-building days have built up impressive berms and platforms out of rebar, wood, and rocks to save the base from being trampled into a sandbox, which is great but it also gives the area a feeling you are climbing in Disneyland and not a State Park. Expect lots of people here and lines for the more coveted routes.

Although the area gets full sun almost all day, the faces of the Dihedrals have varying aspects, so you can chase the shade during warmer times. Unless you want to shred your tips though, you'll likely have to wait awhile for the holds to cool down before giving these thin, technical climbs a go.

The Dihedrals have dozens of routes from 5.6 to 5.14a and are broken up into three sectors: the Right, Center, and Left Dihedrals.

Rio Rose on *Sunshine Dihedral* 5.11d (page 46).

RIGHT DIHEDRALS • KARATE WALL

Forming the far rightside of the Dihedrals, the sheer flank of the Karate Wall is the proud home to a handful of long, super high-quality pitches. If 5.12 edging is what you're after, this is your zone. This is the first of the three main east face walls in the Dihedrals and has a bevy of link-ups and extensions—all of which are excellent.

A few of the pitches are 30+ meters long, so running a 70-meter cord is handy. Even with a 70, you'll barely reach the ground after the belayer has scrambled up the talus a bit, so **always tie a knot in the end of the rope!** The anchors on top of the Karate Wall have unfortunately become a destination to free rappel for kooked-out mountaineering clubs. If anyone is sport rappelling off these anchors, be careful—more than once a clueless individual has rapped right over a climber mid-redpoint.

Besides sport rapellers, heat is the enemy on the Karate Wall as the thin edges and technical moves demand crisp temps in order to prevent your tips from shearing back like banana peel. The wall faces east and goes into the shade by noon, but usually takes longer to cool off after baking in the sun since dawn. This right side of the Dihedrals also hosts some excellent 5.12s that face south and receive a lot more sun than Karate Wall—a nice option on cold, clear winter days when Karate Wall is freezing.

❶ Karate Crack 5.10a ★★★★ ☐
A Smith classic, this stellar pitch of straight-in hands is also the start to four other routes on Karate Wall. The crux is a thin section early on, and the rest is pure hands. Traverse right at the top of the crack—placing some protection on the traverse for your partner—and belay from a bolted anchor in the pod. Bring hand-sized gear.

Although marked as sport climbs, you will need gear for the following routes, Slow Burn, Crossfire, and Power Dive, because you must lead Karate Crack to get to the bolted climbing. Another option is to rap down, clip the first couple of bolts on any of those climbs, and then pull the rope, thereby allowing you to toprope Karate Crack and then lead through the bolts.

❷ Slow Burn 5.11d ★★ ☐
A good line, but pales in comparison to Karate Wall's other routes. Above *Karate Crack*, climb straight up for two bolts, then shoot right up a runout 5.11 face.

❸ Crossfire 5.12b ★★★★ ☐
Absolutely mega. Position, moves, and rock. If you're up for the grade, this is a must-do line. Up *Karate Crack*, then straight to a cruxy thin move at the first bolt. Short people (i.e. all you sub 5'6" midgets) avoid this somewhat reachy crux move by circling around to the left. A second thin crux comes near the top before traversing left to join *Power Dive's* final bolt (hard to clip) and one last pumper crux.

❹ Power Dive 5.12a ★★★★ ☐
From the big hole above *Karate Crack* move left and up a series of thin moves. Hard right before the last bolt, which is difficult to clip. Strangely pumpy for vertical 12a.

❺ Karot Tots 5.11b ★★★ ☐
A cool thin seam that diagonals across the wall from right to left. About a body length before the hand traverse on *Karate Crack*, move left to a bolt and then thin jamming and edges. Belay around the corner at a bolted anchor (hard to see). There is a second pitch to the top of the wall (5.6) but no one wastes their time with it—and neither should you. Bring a selection of thin cams and nuts.

❻ Firing Line 5.12b ★★★★ ☐
A very technical line of thin edges left of *Karate Crack*. A bit runout in spots but the bolts are always where you need them. Link into *Karot Tots'* crack, traversing around the corner to the hard-to-see anchor.

❼ Karate Wall 5.12c ★★★★ ☐
Few routes at Smith pack as much value as this incredible tour up the entire left side of the wall. Basically a combination of *Firing Line* and *Power Dive*, requiring a 70-meter rope to lower. Significantly more demanding and continuous than the neighboring 5.12bs, *Crossfire* and *Latest Rage*. A Rock 4-sized nut placement reduces the runout where you link into *Power Dive*. You get a good shake just below but the pump returns quickly as you battle up the edges to the anchor. Constantly technical, a lead of this 35-meter route commonly takes 30+ minutes, so get comfy if you're belaying—and don't forget to tie a knot in the end of the rope!

❽ Latest Rage 5.12b ★★★★ ☐
The first of several classic arêtes in the Dihedrals and often called the best 12b at Smith. Seems short (it's only four bolts) but packs a punch, never allowing for much recovery. The first bolt is commonly stick clipped. Hard at the last bolt, where light-duty sissies go right avoiding the proper direct finish up the arête. The climbing above the last bolt is no harder than 10a but is mega runout so be sure to keep a cool head.

RIGHT DIHEDRALS, KARATE WALL

⑨ Watts Tots 5.12b ★★

The first rap-bolted sport climb at Smith, this not-that-popular line is all about late 1980s technical less-than-vertical edge climbing. A one-move wonder, with the crux coming as a tricky frag move near the top. A necessary tick for 5.12 climbers looking to taste some of Smith's history, otherwise skip it and have a go on the much better *Latest Rage* or *Crossfire*.

⑩ Freshly Squeezed 5.11a

A lame route squeezed in (thus the punny name) to the left of *Watts Tots*. Hard down low. You can also climb the face to the right of the bolts. This 12b climb *Kilo Watts* used to be a toprope, but now thanks to the bolts on *Freshly Squeezed* you can lead it.

⑪ Trivial Pursuit 5.10d R ★

Another runout moderate route that no one bothers with. The crux is at the second bolt followed by easy knobs with massive spaces betweens the bolts on the upper slab.

⑫ Tater Tots 5.10a R ★

Just like *Trivial Pursuit* only with an easier crux, again at the second bolt. Joins into the runout upper slab of *Trivial Pursuit*.

⑬ Latin Lover 5.12a ★★★

Tucked into the slot around the corner from *Tater Tots*, this heavily-chalked pebble climb is a dream for little hands and a nightmare for men with sausage fingers. A great hideout from the summer heat as it gets shade until later in the day than just about any climb in the Dihedrals. Rather than go straight up at the fifth bolt you can (though almost no one does) step left and continue up unending 5.11+ knobs and pebbles for a giant pitch of technical and mental endurance called *Peepshow*, which bumps the grade by half a notch to 12a/b.

CENTER DIHEDRALS

This sector was Ground Zero for the Smith's sport-climbing explosion in the 1980s. Here's where you'll find Smith's first 5.13a sport climb *Darkness At Noon*, America's first 5.14a *To Bolt Or Not To Be,* and slew of 5.12 testpieces that continue to draw climbers from around the world.

Vertical knobs and edges is the gig here, so be sure to have a stiff pair of shoes in order to dial-in the footwork-intensive climbing. This sector is also one of the most popular in the park, so expect lots of people, especially on the weekends—and double especially on prime ticks like *Heinous Cling.*

① Take a Powder 5.12a ★★★★
Starts off with an easy looking flake that is far from it—more like solid 5.11. Efficiency is the key on the flake because once it peters out the climb's business kicks in on technical micro-knobs. This baby doesn't let up until the anchors.

② Powder In Your Eyes 5.12c ★★
You'll think 5.13 at Smith is impossible if this cryptic route is "only" 12c. Technical climbing up the small arête/corner reached after cutting left at *Take a Powder's* 3rd bolt.

③ Sunshine Dihedral 5.11d ★★★★
A classic stemming corner. The gear is marginal down low, but the crux section is well protected by a couple of bolts, a pin, and bomber gear. A classic stemming testpiece. A second pitch (5.10) continues above but is seldom done.

④ French Connection 5.13b ★★★★
A rope stretcher pitch that climbs *Sunshine Dihedral* to the rest jug on the right face and then cuts left into *To Bolt Or Not To Be* crux sequence at the 9th bolt. From above the crux to the anchors is demanding 12d edge climbing. Difficult and involved.

⑤ To Bolt Or Not To Be 5.14a ★★★★
This is it. The first 5.14a on American soil. An incredible testpiece of technical edge climbing. First climbed in 1986, *To Bolt* is on the hit list of every big-name climber, but (as a testament to its high-involved nature) has seen less than 20 ascents. New anchors have been placed just below the lip of the wall, but you'll still need a 70-meter rope to lower off—and even then the belayer has to scramble up the talus a bit. Be sure to tie a knot in the end of the rope!

⑥ Last Waltz 5.12c ★★★★
Some people have half-seriously called this line 13a—it probably is if you aren't adept at delicate, technical moves. Another line hailed as "the best 12c in the park." Start up *Moondance* and at the third bolt move right (not easy) to a stem rest below the roof. After shaking out sketch up the gorgeous arête via numerous baffling sequences. A mega-classic arête climb. There is also a rarely done direct start that leads straight into the roof, but sports only a single bolt, making for certain groundfall if you blow the 5.12 moves.

⑦ Moondance 5.11c ★★★
A route with two distinct characters. The first half is slabby edges, while the second half (after a rest jug) is complex tick-tack stemming. Luckily the stemming crux comes immediately after the rest jug and eases as you approach the anchor. You can continue above the anchor with more 5.11 climbing (two bolts and a big runout), but then you'll have to rap to get off.

⑧ Wedding Day 5.10b ★★★
One of the few 5.10s in the Dihedrals, so it's quite popular. The start is hard, but it also doesn't really let up until the anchors.

⑨ The Flat Earth 5.12a
A lame line not worth doing. Expect a couple of cruxes and awkward climbing. Shares anchors with *Wedding Day.*

⑩ Middle Aged Vandals 5.11c ★★
Alan Watts was harassed by a new park ranger for "vandalizing" the cliff when he was equipping this route, thus the name. Hard moves are always followed by good rests. A popular second-option warm-up for locals if hordes are lined up on *Heinous Cling.*

⑪ Moonshine Dihedral 5.9 ★★★★
An awesome moderate corner that eats up gear, making for a safe lead. Classic climbing on bullet stone in the heart of the Dihedrals. The needless bolt halfway up has been removed. You can climb junky stone all the way to the top of the wall (5.9) in a single pitch, but most everyone lowers from the first set of anchors.

⑫ Heinous Cling Start 5.12a ★★★★
The most popular 12a in the park—by a factor of 10. This route sees traffic almost every day of the year. And for good reason—it's fantastic. Originally led with two bolts (the 1st and 5th) and micro-gear—now all you need is quickdraws. Solo up the 15 feet of easy crack and then follow the bolts and chalk up thin edges and pockets. A runout at, and above, the crux deadpoint makes for entertaining whipper watching. Short people can get around the deadpoint by using a crafty heel hook. Locals have ruthlessly beta'd down this route and can hike it on demand.

CENTER DIHEDRALS

RIGHT DIHEDRALS

CENTER DIHEDRALS

⑬ Heinous Cling (aka Full Heinous) 5.12c ★★★★☐
Above the 12a *Heinous Start* loom three more bolts
(in 40-plus feet!) that add a significant amount of
value to the pitch. This is the original Henious Cling
line. There's a bolt near the crux (the only bolt on the
upper headwall when the line was first done back in
1984), but the anchor is guarded by a huge runout
on mid-range 5.11 climbing. A fall from the runout
wouldn't be terminal, but it would be extremely
exciting. Another mega-classic Smith Rock 12c. Use a
70-meter cord. Shares anchors with *Darkness*.

⑭ Darkness At Noon 5.13a ★★★★ ☐
The first 13a in the park and still one of the best,
soaring up the entire left side of the wall. Another line
locals have absurdly dialed. The first half is thin and
technical on pockets and edges, while the upper stretch
is steep and pumpy. You can bail off to *Heinous Cling's*
first set of anchors at the 5th bolt, but that dumps the
grade down to 12c. Not as heavily traffic as *Churning*,
but not by much. FYI: the route goes into the shade
at ... you guessed it, noon. Use a 70-meter cord. Same
anchors as *Full Heinous*.

⑮ Chain Reaction 5.12c ★★★★ ☐
Easily the most visually famous sport climb in
America. Show any climber from China to the Czech
Republic to Canada a photo of this stunning, iconic
knife-edge arête and they'll be able to name it in a
second. A mega-classic arête with powerful slapping
moves to a pumpy final throw to a bucket. Skip the
first bolt on the far left—it's for *Evil Sister* not *Chain
Reaction*—and will only add burly rope drag. A couple
of bolts of jug climbing leads to a series of right-handed slaps and a body tensiony arête hug. Most people
find the big throw at the 4th bolt to be the redpoint
crux with a pump, but shorties may have a majorly
tough time getting established on the arête and using
the jug under the roof.

⑯ Evil Sister 5.13b ☐
Should've called it "Ugly, Lame, Waste of Time Sister."
Chain Reaction's neighboring arête fails to compare.
Rarely climbed.

LEFT DIHEDRALS

On this side of the Dihedrals moderate grades abound, making an excellent zone for green leaders and groups. Lower angled and peppered with knobs, many of the climbs are bolted, but easy trad lines also exist. For 5.12 climbers there are two excellent sport climbs on the extreme left side, typically fixed with draws.

LEFT DIHEDRALS

1 Ancylostoma 5.9 ★★ ☐
A fun jaunt up slabby knobs on a column. For a translation of the route name see below.

2 Bookworm 5.7 ★★★★ ☐
One of the most popular 5.7s in the park. Two great pitches—one of crack and one of knobs. Bring large gear for the upper part of the first pitch. Rap the route.
1. 5.7 Ascend the crack to the top of the column to a bolted belay.
2. 5.7 Cruise up the plentiful knobs, joining *Bunny Face* at the 5th bolt.

An ancylostoma is doctor-speak for "hookworm." Yeah, as in the gnarly worms that latch on to your small intestine and feed off your blood. Females hatch an estimated 10,000 to 25,000 eggs a day, which are then passed through your feces. Yummy.

3 Bunny Face 5.7 ★★★★ ☐
Also one of the most popular 5.7s in the park. Great knob climbing. From the top anchors, rap to *Bookworm's* anchors and then the ground.
1. 5.7 Cruxy moves right off the ground then follow the knobs up to a ledge.
2. 5.7 Step right and surf more knobs up the slab.

4 Methuselah's Column 5.10a R ☐
A direct finish to *Bunny Face* or *Rabbit Stew* that is horribly runout and chossy. Avoid at all costs.

5 Rabbit Stew 5.7 ★★★ ☐
The left side crack of the *Bunny Face* column requires thin to medium gear to lead, but is often toproped from the *Bunny Face* anchors. A good introductory trad lead for 5.7 climbers.

6 Lycopodophyta 5.7 ★★★ ☐
A more sustained (and some say better) corner than *Rabbit Stew*. Bring small cams and nuts for the lead. There is a second pitch but it's a wide, nasty affair that's not worth putting yourself through the trauma

for. BTW: For all of you non-botanists, lycopodophyta is plant-hugger speak for a specific strain of moss.

7 Helium Woman 5.9 ★★ ☐
Hard moves down low yield to low-angle knobs.

8 Captain Xenolith 5.10a ★★ ☐
This sister route to *Helium Woman* also has its crux down low. The rest is much easier.

9 Go Dog Go 5.12c ★★★★ ☐
The crux comes in one of two spots, depending on your climbing style. Low on the slab is a tricky "softball" hold that spits many people off—especially if it's in the sun. High in the steeps is a major lock-off on a two-finger pocket. Luckily you're punching for a bucket. A great and varied route with outstanding position.

10 Vision 5.12b ★★★★ ☐
A cool arête forming the far rightside of the Dihedrals. Shares its starting bolts with *Go Dog Go* and then bust left to the arête. Technical and fairly steep on pockets and edges.

BW Ropes and Pads —Always between you and the ground.
BlueWater
770-834-7515
www.bluewaterropes.com
Boone Speed Photo

Ian Caldwell on *Scarface* 5.14a (page 52).

6

CHRISTIAN BROTHERS

Bad news for all you bible thumpers out there—the formation's name comes not from any holy foundation or need to hail the wonders of Christianity, but rather as a tribute to the brand of super-low-budj wine you can buy in gallon jugs for $8.99 at the supermarket. Luckily the climbing doesn't reflect a similar lack of quality.

The Christian Brothers stretch all the way from the Dihedrals to Asterix Pass, and has dozens and dozens of quality pitches from spitting-easy 5.5s to finger-wrecking 5.14s, including *Scarface* the first 14a established by an American. The formation is broken up into three main sectors: the Prophet Wall, Testament Slab, and Combination Blocks. The majority of the climbing here is moderate single pitch trad and sport, except for the Prophet Wall where 5.12 and up sport climbs are the deal. The formation loses sun by noon to early afternoon (the east-facing Prophet Wall is the first to get shade), making the Christian Brothers a great spot to head for once the day heats up.

The formation has five main summits (the Abbot, Pope, Friar, Monk, and Priest) but few people actually bother with ticking them because of the high level of choss cloaking their upper flanks. That said, the entire traverse of the five summits (from left to right) makes for an outstanding day of adventure if that sort of endeavor strikes you as fun. Check out Alan Watts' comprehensive guidebook for the full beta and make sure you do it on a winter weekday when no one is likely to be below you to get pummeled by your rain of choss.

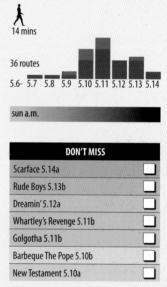

14 mins

36 routes

5.6- 5.7   5.8   5.9   5.10 5.11 5.12 5.13 5.14

sun a.m.

DON'T MISS	
Scarface 5.14a	☐
Rude Boys 5.13b	☐
Dreamin' 5.12a	☐
Whartley's Revenge 5.11b	☐
Golgotha 5.11b	☐
Barbeque The Pope 5.10b	☐
New Testament 5.10a	☐

PROPHET WALL

❶ Deep Splash 5.11d ★
Tucked up on the far right side of the Prophet Wall, this manky route is best left alone. A bouldery opening section yields to abysmally loose rock.

❷ La Shootist 5.12c/d ★
A very bouldery start leads to pumpy climbing, a shake on the arête, and then more pumpy climbing. Great position, bad route!

❸ Chemical Ali 5.14a ★★★
Ali Hassan al-Majid known as "Chemical Ali," a cousin of Saddam Hussein, and the man thought to have ordered the 1988 chemical attack on Kurds, is where this stout testpiece gets its name. Al-Majid was the king of spades in the deck of cards issued by the military and No. 5 on the list of the 55 most-wanted Iraqis during Bush's ill-informed attack to find weapons of mass destruction in 2003. First ascentionist Scott Milton (who's Canadian—hey, go find your own war to name routes after!) rated this unrepeated (as of 2005) line 14a, but those who have tried it say it's at least a notch harder. Steep and powerful with numerous 5.13 cruxes. Same start as for *La Shootist* before punching it left at the 2nd bolt.

❽ Boy Prophet 5.12b ★★
Shares the same start as *Dreamin'*, then busts left into the finishing slab of *Rude Boys*. The original route on the wall. The upper nut on *Rude Boys* is almost always fixed. Without it you would face a 30+ foot run to the anchors.

❾ Rude Boys 5.13b/c ★★★★
One of the most photographed lines from the early '90s, thanks to the Euro-esque cross-through "rose" move down low. Two boulder problem cruxes, one at the first bolt and the redpoint crux at the bulge. Once you power through to the slab, get tuned in for the mental crux—super runout 5.11 slab climbing with little to no chalk to guide you along. For full value, don't hyper-wire the slab (as many light-duty climbers do) and instead onsight it on your redpoint. A small nut (almost always fixed) provides protection above the final bolt.

❿ Rude Femmes 5.13c ★★
A very rarely done variant finish to *Rude Boys*. At the fourth bolt step left and voyage up the endless, runout slab that makes *Rude Boys'* slab look like a clip-up. You'll need a 70-meter cord to lower off.

> "Ali Hassan al-Majid known as 'Chemical Ali' ... was the king of spades in the deck of cards issued by the military and No. 5 on the list of the 55 most-wanted Iraqis during Bush's ill-informed attack to find weapons of mass destruction in 2003. First ascentionist Scott Milton (who's Canadian—*hey*, go find your own war to name routes after!) rated this unrepeated (as of 2005) line 14a, but those who have tried it say it's at least a notch harder."

❹ Rawhide 5.11d ★★
A mostly traversing line on very small holds with even smaller feet. The first bolt is commonly stick clipped and the business is around the third bolt.

❺ Smooth Boy 5.13b ★★
A tricky route with a crux coming via a powerful and thin sequence over the roof at the 5th bolt. The vertical wall below (5.12) and above the crux (5.11) is technical and involved.

❻ Choke On This 5.13a ★★
Vertical funkness on excellent rock for the first three bolts leads to a couple of overlaps and 5.11 slab finish.

❼ Dreamin' 5.12a ★★★★
A mega-classic line with bold runouts. Easily identified by the stacks of chalk covering the route. The technical crux is a delicate sequence at the third bolt, but the route gets its character from the runout 5.11 slab above. Full-value climbing—make sure you have your head dialed-in. Many find pulling the roof to be the redpoint crux.

⓫ Scarface 5.14a ★★★★
Another of Smith's historic climbs for two reasons. Number One—it was the first 14a established by an American, Scott Franklin (Congratulations, Scott!). Number Two—an ice tool was used to pry off a flake at the 6th bolt that would have provided too good of a rest for the climb to be 14a. Once downgraded to 13d (Sorry, Scott!), the consensus grade has once again returned to 14a (Congratulations, Scott!). A mono move at the third bolt is nasty hard, but most find the redpoint crux to be pulling the roof. Use a 70-meter rope.

⓬ Shoes Of The Fisherman 5.11b
An unpopular, though good-looking, steep crack. The awkward, dirty climbing keeps traffic to a minimum, especially with the classic *Wartley's Revenge* so close to the left. If you really gotta do this line bring small to hand-sized gear. The route goes to the top via 5.8 trash but even those foolish enough to do the first part of this marginal route don't go any further than the first set of anchors.

MOST EPIC REDPOINT

Winner of the "Most Epic Redpoint In Smith Rock's History" goes to Chris Knuth who surprised himself while working Rude Boys and got through the cruxes only to find himself on the three-bolt slab with only one quickdraw on his harness. Knuth coolly broke down the quickdraw for two biners, scarfed a third biner from his toothbrush, and used them as single biners on the three bolts, punching past the nut placement to the anchors. Good job. But one problem —he was now a solid 30+ feet runout and had nothing to clip into the anchor with. Knuth, in a shockingly bold "are-you-fricking-insane" move, hooked his leg through the anchor webbing, untied, and threaded the rope through the anchor. Now *that's* a redpoint!

⓭ **Heresy (aka 20 Feet of Trying)** 5.11d ★★ ☐
A silly, obscenely short route that inexplicably draws traffic. Stays dry in the rain though, unlike 90-percent of the climbing at Smith. Powerful jug hauling to a crux bit right before the anchors. Lower off, or, if you have a crashpad, jump.

⓮ **Wartley's Revenge** 5.11b ★★★★ ☐
One of the best 5.11 crack pitches at Smith. A stemmy section down low leads into absolutely classic jamming and flake jugs out a bulge. The pump adds up until the final lock-off move to the anchor bucket. Locals have this route completely wired (cracks too?!) and have the rack dialed down to the bare minimum. For everyone else, be sure to bring a full selection of small to medium gear. The route keeps going up easy 5.10 but the rock is loose and crappy so everyone lowers from the first set of anchors.

TESTAMENT SLAB

1 Golgotha 5.11b ★★★★

The excellent corner just to the right of *Barbeque The Pope*. Locker jams protected by bomber nuts lead into a two-bolt section of tricky stemming.

2 Barbeque The Pope 5.10b ★★★★

One of the most popular 5.10s in the park. Classic Smith edging that is incredibly pumpy. More than few people have (or nearly have) decked out getting the 3rd bolt clipped. Blame erosion for the extra high first bolt.

3 New Testament 5.10a ★★★★

A fun, straight-in hand crack. No move is too hard, just continuous jamming. Bring medium to hand-sized gear.

4 Revelations 5.9 ★★

A pleasant ramble up the slab's arête. Plenty of knobs keep the grade moderate. Easier the higher you get. A touch runout to the first bolt, so many people finagle a nut in down low.

5 Irreverence 5.10a ★★★

The bolted line in the center of the face. Smaller knobs (especially around the third bolt) make it a touch harder than *Revelations*. Joins up with *Revelations* for the last two bolts.

6 Nightingale's On Vacation 5.10a ★★

Ascends the left arête of the Testament slab. Tricky climbing as evidenced by the common sight of bail biners on the upper half of the climb. Cruxy at the 4th bolt.

7 Blasphemy 5.11a ★★

Over bolted stemming to the left of the giant chimney. Finishes via easy ledges.

8 Panic Attack 5.12a ★★

Similar to *Blasphemy* only a full grade harder and even more over bolted (the bolts are so close together—sometimes only two-feet apart—you can easily z-clip).

CHRISTIAN BROTHERS • TESTAMENT SLAB

COMBINATION BLOCKS

1 Private Trust 5.11c ★ ☐
A seldom done two-bolt line just to the right of the Combination Blocks. Big run to the first bolt. After the bolts, slither into the block's chasm or lay away the outside.

2 Overnight Sensation 5.11a ★ ☐
Straightforward 5.10 climbing to a small ledge. Above the ledge is a stopper boulder problem at the fourth bolt. Shorter people are unable to clip the bolt off the ledge and therefore face a potential ledge fall if the crux is botched. After a busy weekend you're almost guaranteed to find a bail biner on this route.

3 Double Trouble 5.10b ★★ ☐
A fun arête climb on the left side of the Combination Blocks. No move is stopper, but the sustained layaways give climbers fits.

4 Double Stain 5.13a ★★ ☐
A historically significant route (it was Smith's first 5.13), this thin RP seam on the wall above the Combination Blocks sees little traffic. The crux is tip-jamming in pinned out scars with micro nuts for gear. Approach via any of the Combination Blocks' routes.

5 Bum Rush The Show 5.13b ★★ ☐
Another obscure 5.13 atop the Combination Blocks. Hard moves down low sap enough strength to make the 5.12 finish a battle of pump management. Lots of glue.

6 Toys In The Attic 5.9 ★★ ☐
The hand crack in the corner to the left of Combination Blocks. Right below the roof (crux), traverse left to the anchors atop *Hesitation Blues*. Bring medium to big-hands-sized gear.

7 Child's Play 5.10c ★★ ☐
A variation finish to *Toys In The Attic*. After 30 feet, branch left into a thin crack that leads directly to the anchor. Requires thin gear to lead, or simply top rope the line.

8 Hesitation Blues 5.10b ★★★ ☐
The fixed pins down low have been replaced with bolts, but the climbing is still demanding and pumpy. Use small and medium gear.

9 Attic Antics 5.11b ★★ ☐
A great, albeit short, extension to *Hesitation Blues*. Reach past the anchors, pull over the scrunchy roof and work the thin locks and stems. Protect by two bolts, then just run it out on easy ground to the *Jete/Dancer* anchors.

10 Ring Of Fire 5.11c/d ★★ ☐
A marginal route that is for some reason extremely popular. Easy edges lead to a stopper sequence of underclings and edges with techy feet at the third eye-bolt.

11 Name Unknown 5.10a ★ ☐
An easier bolted line immediately to the left of *Ring Of Fire*. The lower section of climbing wanders a fair bit and many people stay far to the left, avoiding the awkward cruxy knobs. Can be linked into the finish of *Ring Of Fire* for a mid-5.10 grade.

12 Toy Blocks 5.10a ★★ ☐
The crack cutting left to right across the face. Either finish up a 5.8 hand crack or keep traversing (5.10) to the *Hesitation Blues* anchor for a super-girdle of the face. Medium to hand-sized gear needed.

13 Dancer 5.7 ★★★ ☐
A great moderate face climb on knobs. Well bolted and slabby, it makes a great lead for those breaking into 5.7 leading. Gets hard right after the ramp.

14 Jete 5.8 ★★★ ☐
Another great intro lead for 5.7-5.8 climbers. Nearly identical to *Dancer* in quality and difficulty. Tricky down low, though, so make sure your belayer is ready to prevent a groundfall. Joins *Dancer* above the fourth bolt.

WHERE THE INTERNET ROCKS

SmithRock.com

7

PHOENIX BUTTRESS

Requiring the longest walk of the frontside areas, this small buttress is stacked with quality 5.9 to 5.11 climbing on extremely solid, yet exceptionally sharp at times, red and purple rock. Simply stroll alongside the Crooked River, passing literally all of the frontside climbing until this clean wall is reached directly off the trail.

Phoenix Buttress is a nice diversion from the heat and dust of the other frontside areas. Juniper, sage, and pine trees give the area a relaxing "backside" feel. The wall receives loads of shade, typically losing sun by noon, making it a perfect spot to head to for some fun 5.11-and-under climbing on a hot day. It's also a great people-watching spot, as you can scope-out the love, lust, and hate going on from Testament Slab all the way to Morning Glory Wall.

18 mins

7 routes

5.6- 5.7   5.8   5.9   5.10 5.11 5.12 5.13 5.14

sun a.m.

DON'T MISS	
JT's Route 5.10b	☐
Phoenix 5.10a	☐

PHOENIX BUTTRESS

1 Drill'em and Fill'em 5.10a ★★
The furthest right route. Starts off giant flake. Cruxy down low, cruiser (but a touch runout) up high. Tied for fifth best route on the cliff.

2 Phoenix 5.10a ★★★
Varied climbing on pockets and edges. Technical moves on small holds. Best route on the cliff.

3 License to Bolt 5.11b ★★
Difficult start with bad feet. Strenuous climbing all the way to the anchors. Third best route on the cliff.

4 Fred On Air 5.10d ★★
A wandering opening section leads to straightforward edging and pockets. Fourth best route on the cliff.

5 JT's Route 5.10b ★★★
Yee-ouch! Smart stemming will take most of the pain out of grabbing this route's sharp holds. The well-bolted finishing crux bulge makes this a great route for aspiring 5.10b leaders. Second best route on the cliff.

6 Hissing Llamas 5.8 ★★
Moderate slab climbing with plenty of bolts. Another great lead for aspiring leaders. Tied for fifth best route on cliff.

7 When Llamas Bolt 5.11a ★
Slab climbing leads to an awkward arête. Looks cool but climbs like crap. Worst route on the cliff.

8
MESA VERDE BUTTRESS

Sick of the crowds and heat of the frontside? Head over Asterisk Pass and leave 'em behind at this secluded and shady wall absolutely stacked with stellar sport and trad lines. To be honest, most of the climbing at Smith's "backside" is fairly marginal with the quality pitches widely spread out amongst the many walls and crags—the exception is the towering Mesa Verde, a primo wall for 5.11-and-under climbers, housing such mega-classics as the otherworldly knobs-forever arête of *Moons of Pluto* (5.10d) and *Trezlar's* luscious 5.10a stemming dihedral. Facing west, the wall is cloaked in shade until mid to late afternoon, making it a perfect crag for the hotter months.

The best (and fastest) approach to Mesa Verde is via Asterisk Pass. Gain the pass by walking past the climbing on the Christian Brothers area and up towards the "Asterisk"—a 15 foot high boulder that looks like Snoopy's head in profile. After sketching down the west side via a third-class scramble, it's a 10-15 minute walk skirting the base of the back side's other walls to Mesa Verde's easily recognized clean flank 150 yards to the right of *Monkey Face* spire. If you have a dog and/or kids and/or extra time and/or are unnerved by third-classing, Mesa Verde can also be reached via the Misery Ridge trail up to, and down past, Monkey Face (45 minutes from the parking lot) as well as by following the River Trail all the way around past Phoenix Buttress to the backside—a beautiful stroll that takes about an hour from the parking lot.

There are a few random routes on the wall's far right side, all of which suck. The massive 350-foot central face is as blank as it looks, yielding only an old bang-and-conquer aid climb (*Palo Verde* 5.6 A3). All of the good climbing is located on the left side, beginning around a lonely juniper tree near the lowest point of the wall.

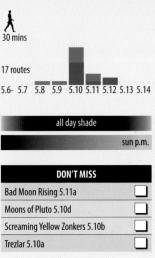

30 mins

17 routes

| 5.6- | 5.7 | 5.8 | 5.9 | 5.10 | 5.11 | 5.12 | 5.13 | 5.14 |

all day shade
sun p.m.

DON'T MISS	
Bad Moon Rising 5.11a	☐
Moons of Pluto 5.10d	☐
Screaming Yellow Zonkers 5.10b	☐
Trezlar 5.10a	☐

MESA VERDE BUTTRESS

1 Cows In Agony 5.10d ★
Harder if you stay to the right (like 11a-ish) at mid-height—but why would you when the good holds are over left? Tough moves at the top.

2 Cliff Dwelling Crack 5.8 ★★
Some fun liebacking. Bring the big cams—this baby gets awfully wide up high.

3 Juniper Face 5.12a ★★
The face behind the juniper tree (duh). Bring your stiff shoes and a full bag of technical skills. Cruxy in the middle.

4 Chimney De Chelly 5.10a ★★
First, it's not "shelly." It's "shay"—as in a play on Canyon De Chelly National Monument. Second, if you can't find this massive dihedral cutting up the wall, you're hopeless. Third, this multi-pitch trad line has three pitches—two are good (the first and third), one is bad (the second!). Fourth, bring mostly small to medium sized gear. Fifth, to descend, scramble along the ledge until reaching the *Trezlar* anchor and rap off via one double-rope rappel or walk off (hassle) to the north via sketchy ledges.
1. 5.10 Thin jamming (bolt) to easy climbing and a traverse out right to a bolted anchor.
2. 5.9 Give this junk show pitch to your partner. A bolt protects the hardest bit of climbing. Loose and crumbly up high.
3. 5.8 A quality pitch of corner jamming leads to an easy (and clean!) chimney.

5 Desolation Row 5.11a ★★★
If you're up for the challenge, this makes for a great alternative to the lame second pitch of *Chimney De Chelly*. Bring small to medium gear. Descent is the same as for *Chimney De Chelly*.
1. 5.11a Start on *Chimney De Chelly*, but continue straight up instead of traversing right. Awkward jamming leads into a cruxy liebacking section pulling around the roof—fortunately there's a bolt at the hard bit.
2. 5.8 Same as the third pitch of *Chimney De Chelly*.

6 Shadow Of Doubt 5.12a ★★
No stopper moves just five bolts of continuous 5.11 climbing before bailing left to the anchor.

7 Reason To Be 5.10d ★★★
Cool arête climbing at a doable grade. Nice stone. Left hand works the arête while right hand crimps small edges. Shares same anchor as *Shadow Of Doubt*.

8 Tale Of Two Shitties 5.10a ★★★
Another awesome Mesa Verde 5.10, this time a three-pitch tour with lots of variety and quality rock. Same rack and descent as for *Chimney De Chelly*.
1. 5.7 Jam up the broken crack system, starting just uphill from the wall's lowest point. Set up gear anchor below the obvious dihedral.
2. 5.10a Sweet pitch of jamming on stellar rock. Hard up high. Move right after the bulge to a bolted anchor.
3. 5.9 Three bolts of balancey climbing leads into cruiser knobs.

9 Sundown 5.9 ★★★
Thin jamming in a dihedral. Nice pitch. Takes small to medium gear.

10 Down's Syndrome 5.10a ★★
An airy continuation of *Sundown*. From *Sundown's* anchors continue straight up and left on knobs. A touch sporty for a 5.10 leader. Shares anchor with the second pitch of *Minas Morgul*.

11 Minas Morgul 5.11d ★★
A seldom done three–pitcher due to the marginal first pitch and the demanding second pitch. Can be alternatively started with *Sundown* as the first pitch. The first and second pitch can both be avoided by doing *Down's Syndrome*. The first, second, and third pitch can all be avoided by staying on the ground. Need mostly small to medium gear. Same descent as *Chimney De Chelly's*.
1. 5.8 Start by face climbing on the large block leaning against the wall. Finish up crappy stone to an awkward belay. Can combine with second pitch.
2. 5.11d Pumpy jams to an even pumpier roof sequence.
3. 5.9 Great climbing up an easy crack to a cruxy finger crack.

12 Bad Moon Rising 5.11a ★★★★
An awesome face climb easily identified by the stack of cheater stones at the reachy, technical start. After scratching through the start follow continuous knobs to an extremely pumpy crux roof. Make sure to knot the end of the rope while lowering—you just barely reach the ground with a 60.

13 Moons Of Pluto 5.10d ★★★★
One of the best 5.10s at Smith. Endless micro-knobs up a laser-cut arête. Cruxy at the top. A must-do. When lowering with a 60-meter cord, don't forget to tie a knot in the end of the rope!

14 Screaming Yellow Zonkers 5.10b ★★★★
Another super-mega 5.10. As good (some say better) than *Moons of Pluto*. A classic line cruising up knobs and pockets. Same start as *Moons of Pluto* but at the first bolt angles left. Shares anchor with *Moons of Pluto* so make sure to tie that knot in the end of the rope!

REDPOINT
975 NE SMITHROCK WA
TERREBONNE, OR 97760
541-923-6207

BATCH# 134
S-A-L-E-S D-R-A-F-T
73827793
009503824956

REF: 0903
CD TYPE: VISA
TR TYPE: PURCHASE
INV:
DATE: APR 14, 09 09:54:00

TOTAL $19.95

ACCT: ***********5319   EXP: **/**
AP: 145548
NAME: MAURICE C BAKER

CARDMEMBER ACKNOWLEDGES RECEIPT OF GOODS
AND/OR SERVICES IN THE AMOUNT OF THE
TOTAL SHOWN HEREON AND AGREES TO PERFORM
THE OBLIGATIONS SET FORTH BY THE
CARDMEMBER'S AGREEMENT WITH THE ISSUER

THANKS FOR USING VISA

X _____

TOP COPY-MERCHANT BOTTOM COPY-CUSTOMER

Renan Ozturk on *North Face* 5.12a (page 66).

MONKEY FACE • WEST FACE

The west face gets afternoon sun and has the most popular route to the summit, *West Face Variation*, a four pitch 5.8 with an AO bolt ladder. Other classics include *Astro Monkey*, with its stellar cracks, and the outrageously exposed 5.11b face climbing of *Monkey Space*.

❶ West Face Variation 5.8 A0 ★★★★ ☐
The most popular line to the summit of the Monkey, this is actually a two-pitch direct start to the Monkey's original summit route, the *Pioneer Route*. Though the grade is light-duty, exposed climbing and a steep bolt ladder make this route not a good option for novices. The bolt ladder especially is a common scene of newbie epics. Have your aiding and jugging dialed before tackling this amazing line. You'll need small to medium gear for the first two pitches and then it's bolts the rest of the way.

1. 5.7 Start up a steep flake/bulge directly in front of the Search and Rescue backboard litter. Jam an easier corner and belay from either of the two bolted anchors on the ramp.
2. 5.8 There are many variations to gain the *Bohn Street* belay ledge below the bolt ladder. This is the best and most straightforward: Step left onto a slab to gain a stellar flare with finger locks. Wander up easy terrain until you reach the notch. Shoot up to *Bohn Street* via a wide crack, using face holds when things get wide and burly.
3. A0 Head directly up the bolt ladder to the east cave. Awkward getting into the cave. The bolt line has gone free at hard 5.13 but most climbers will be happy just to aid the plentiful bolts. About halfway up the ladder there's a line of four bolts to the right that goes free at 12d (called *Young Pioneers*) but it's rarely done.
4. 5.7 Is this the most exposed 5.7 in America? Hmm ... you be the judge. Dubbed "Panic Point," the wild step out the east side of the cave yields instant exposure over what feels like 1500 feet of air (it's actually only about 150). The first few moves are the hardest, which adds to the intimidation factor. The bolts are super close together so if you get freaked you can just aid the pitch or grab draws. After 20 feet the exposure relents and there is an anchor at the Monkey's "nose" boulder (this is the rap anchor for the free rappel). If you want to get photos of your second pulling around "Panic Point" stop here, otherwise it's best to skip this anchor and just continue over or around the boulder and up the easy climbing to the final anchor immediately below the summit.
4a. 5.8 A bolted variation on the Panic Point experience that extends the exposure by angling up and right rather than heading straight up to the Monkey's nose. This great variation deserves more traffic.

❷ Monkey Space 5.11b ★★★★ ☐
A wildly exposed face climb off of *Bohn Street*. One of the best 5.11s at Smith. Absolutely classic. Gain *Bohn Street* via *West Face Variation* or the *Pioneer Route*.

1. 5.11a Follow the bolts leading out left from *Bohn Street*. Cruxy pulling the bulge. Some people may want a cam to protect the final 10 feet of easy flake crack leading into the massive west cave. Amazing position.
2. 5.11b Move the belay to the north (left) side of the cave and then climb the steep, short headwall. After pulling the headwall, easy ground leads to anchors below the summit. Very powerful for the grade.

❸ Drug Nasty 5.11c ☐
A scabby line that sees little to zero traffic. Skip this pile and have a go on either of the two excellent pitches just to its left.

❹ Moving In Stereo 5.11d ★★★ ☐
A great pitch with a variety of moves. Easily identified by its rusty hangers and left-facing offset. Cruxy getting into the crack. A popular variation to the testy first pitch of *Astro Monkey*.

❺ Astro Monkey 5.11d ★★★★ ☐
An outstanding five-pitch route (though pales dramatically in comparison to its namesake route in Yosemite) highlighted by the overhanging third pitch corner. You'll need small to medium gear for the first three pitches and then it's bolts to the summit via *Monkey Space*.

1. 5.11d A stout pitch of bolt-protected micro pebbles and edges that lead into a pumpy crack around a roof. Skip the first set of anchors and continue up easy terrain to the second anchors.
2. 5.9 Locker finger locks up a crack splitting a clean face. Belay below the overhanging corner.
3. 5.11a A classic pitch of steep jams and laybacks up the overhanging dihedral with a single bolt in the roof. Easier than it looks. Near the top of the corner you can surf right past a lip bolt to easy ground leading up to *Bohn Street*. The original way is to go left at the top of the corner and tackle another thin corner out a roof and up to *Bohn Street*. The problem with going the original way is dealing with the rope drag and that the crack in the upper roof is a notorious rope sucker—no matter how careful you are with rope it'll get jammed. You have been warned.
4. & 5. Climb *Monkey Space*.

DESCENT

Getting down from the top of the spire requires two ropes. First make a short single-rope rap from the anchor just below the summit to the small stance at the Monkey's "nose" just above the east cave. From here it's a super-airy free-hanging double-rope rappel to the base of the east face. Use a rap glove and/or a prussik back-up if you're intimidated by exposed raps—this is as wild of a rappel as you'll find at Smith.

WEST FACE (RIGHT)

6 Pose Down 5.12c ★★ ☐

A super technical start (especially around the second bolt) leads to continuous 11+ climbing. You can avoid the desperate start by aiding in from the bolts on *West Face* and reduce the grade to 12a.

7 West Face 5.12a A0 ★★★★ ☐

A proud line punching up the blank upper section of the west face via an incredibly long bolt ladder. Numerous bolts have been replaced on the onetime sketchy ladder, thereby reducing the fear factor. Bring small to medium gear for the first pitch.

1. 5.12a A0 Yard through the A0 start and then plug into the finger crack. A long, hard pitch finishing with more bolts, this time freeable at 5.11. You can make the pitch even harder (12b) by avoiding the A0 moves and linking in from the start of *Sheer Trickery*.
2. A0 Hard to get off route here—just aid up the endless line of bolts. Cool position on the blank headwall. Belay on a small ledge.
3. 5.12a Another stout pitch of heads-up 12a, this time on bolts. Exposed and technical. Doesn't let up until you mantle into the west cave.
4. 5.11b Same finish as for *Monkey Space*. A burly finish to a burly climb.

8 Sheer Trickery 5.12b ★★★ ☐

Another stout 5.12 on the Monkey. This one starts via bolted face climbing on the far leftside of the west face then avoids a blank section by linking into the West Face's 5.11 crack before busting back to four more bolts of 5.12 face climbing on the arête. A double rope rap from a bolted anchor around the corner will get you off or you can significantly up the ante by multi-pitching into *The Backbone* or the *North Face*.

WEST FACE (LEFT)

MONKEY FACE • NORTH AND EAST FACES

The east and north faces of the spire are home to one of America's most famed 5.14 sport climbs, *Just Do It*, and Smith's best 5.12 crack the *North Face*. These faces receive minimal to zero sun, making them perfect for warm days.

⑨ The Backbone 5.13a ★★★★ ☐
A mega-classic arête climb that goes on forever. Exposed, technical, and not for the faint of heart.
1. 5.6 Scramble in from the east side. Not a good warm-up for the burliness ahead.
2. 5.13a Battle up the wildly overhanging double arêtes. It is possible to dodge off line and sneak rests on small ledges. Desperate and airy.
3. 5.12a Same pitch as for *West Face*.
4. 5.12b Exit out the right side of the west cave via long moves on good holds.

⑩ North Face 5.12a ★★★★ ☐
Unquestionably the best 5.12 crack climb at Smith. The second pitch is the business—a 60-meter stretch of pumpy locks and technical stemming. That rope'll feel as heavy as steel cable when you try to clip gear near the top of the pitch. Amazing position with delux rock quality. Bring small to medium gear, especially nuts for the upper pins scars.
1. 5.6 Same easy pitch as for *The Backbone*.
2. 5.12a Intimidating hard face moves protected by bolts right off the belay lead to sinker 5.10 flake jams and laybacks. Once you get past the old hanging belay the difficulties steadily increase as the angle steepens and the jams peter out. The crux kicks in where the rock changes color from tan to red. At the top, traverse right and mantel into the west cave.
3. 5.11b Same finishing pitch as #2 *Monkey Space*.

⑪ Spank The Monkey 5.12a/5.13d ★★★ ☐
A classic arête climb with plenty of air and intimidation. Bolts are always near the hard climbing, but otherwise expect to run out it. Tommy Caldwell recently completed the long forgotten extension to *Spank The Monkey* that continues all the way up the arête. Runout and scary (the rope runs around the arête so much that Caldwell redpointed the line on double ropes), this full pitch checks in at 13d. Enjoy.

⑫ East Face 5.13d ★★★★ ☐
When Alan Watts freed this grievously thin and technical pin-scarred crack in 1985 it was the hardest route in North America. With difficulties near the world maximum, no one really cared that he had freed the pitch with pre-placed gear. Nearly 20 years later, in 2004, Canadian Sonnie Trotter set the bar a notch higher by freeing the pitch while placing gear on lead. Pushing the bar even higher, Trotter, risking 60-footers if he fell, skipped the bolts high on the route, wanting to make a purely trad ascent of the crack. If you want to have a easy sample of this famed crack climb but can't muster the guns for 5.13+ tip jamming, you're in luck—it's "only" 12c to the first set of anchors. A

final 5.10 pitch goes to the Monkey's summit. For gear, bring loads of jumbo fist-size cams, Big Bros, #11 Hexes ... oh and maybe a couple of RP's.

⑬ Just Do It 5.14b ★★★★ ☐
Sport climbs in America don't get more famous than this incredible line. Long, steep, intimidating and technical—the full monty. Although a dark history surrounds the route (i.e. chipping, enhancing, gluing) it has done little to affect the route's status as one of America's finest 5.14s. After massive amounts of work France's J.B. Tribout scored the first ascent in 1992, calling it 14c. The line has now been climbed in less than a handful of tries and has seen its grade settle at 14b. A critical resumé tick for any aspiring hardperson. Make sure to get a custom 90-meter cord from your rope sponsor in order to lower off.

⑭ Megalithic 5.12d ★★ ☐
A distraction of a climb that gets two stars solely because of its rock quality and setting.

⑮ Rising Expectations 5.11d ★★★★ ☐
An outstanding finger crack that provides a solid pump. Thin jams down low sap just enough strength to make the finishing layaway moves the crux. Carry small to medium gear.

⑯ Pioneer Route 5.7 A0 ★★★ ☐
First climbed in 1960, this was the original route to the Monkey's summit. Most people now skip this route's drab start in favor of the much better *West Face Variation*. You'll need a few pieces of medium sized gear for the first 100 feet of climbing to *Bohn Street* and from then on it's bolts to the summit. The real climbing starts 40 feet below the notch, although some people may be a bit unnerved by the exposed 4th classing to the base of the Monkey and may want to rope up earlier.
1. 5.7 A short corner with good stems and locks leads to a wide-ish crack (use face holds when it gets too fat for hand jams) on the west face. A brief bit of face climbing protected by an old bolt gets you to *Bohn Street*.
2-3. Same pitches as the *West Face Variation*—a A0 bolt ladder and the dizzying exposure of the Panic Point pitch. See the *West Face Variation* description (previous page) for full pitch details.

⑰ Close Shave 5.12c ★★ ☐
This climb up the Monkey's neck and chin may seem impossible without trick beta. Watch your rope on the sharp arete. Starts off of *Bohn Street* and finishes up Panic Point.

10 NORTHERN POINT

🚶 7 mins

14 routes

5.6- 5.7 5.8 5.9 5.10 5.11 5.12 5.13 5.14

sun a.m.

DON'T MISS	
A Woman In The Meadow 5.11a	
Limbo 5.11a	

Wanna get your cragging fix and score some pitches quickly? Head to the Northern Point where you can easily bag a half dozen pitches in 30 minutes. The cliff here is around 50 feet tall, approached from above via a cruiser 100-yard walk, and nearly every route has easily accessed anchors on top making it a breeze to rig topropes.This guide covers the two best sectors of climbing, but there are several other lesser climbs spread along the wall, especially cracks. The majority of the climbing profiled here is well-bolted sport climbs that are more gymnastic than the vertical knob and pockets of Smith Rock proper. The wall faces east and loses sun early in the day—a nice option during the heat, but freezing cold on wintry days.

Park for the Northern Point at the end of the Crooked River road about a quarter mile beyond the main Smith Rock parking area. To reach the base of the cliff, hike north toward the "point" of the rimrock and scramble down a 3rd-class gully. Tip for finding the gully: if you look down from the rim and see a dead tree leaning on the wall below you, you're too far to the right. You can also circle around west to east if the gully seems too dicey. There are numerous moderate lines from 5.6 and above to the far left of the descent gully (as you are looking down from the top), making a great zone for climbing classes and beginners

NORTHERN POINT (RIGHT)

NORTHERN POINT (LEFT)

❶ A Woman In The Meadow 5.11a ★★★★ ☐
Roughly 100 yards upriver of the descent gully is this heavily chalked sport climb. Very popular. Positive holds lead to a funky crux at the small triangle-shaped roof.

❷ The Heathen 5.13a ★★★ ☐
Powerful moves through a steep bulge characterize this super-stout route. Rumors of Tommy Caldwell and Jim Karn getting shut down on the crux sequence puts things into perspective.

❸ Made In The Rain 5.12c/d ★★ ☐
Quality liebacking just to the left of *The Heathen*. This route ain't no gimme either, but attracts gym climbers with marginal technique who get shut down on 5.12s in the Dihedrals.

❹ Shiva 5.12b ★ ☐
No chalk and a notoriously reachy crux move keep most people off of this climb. Starts with a cool jumbo-flake lieback though.

❺ Limbo 5.11a ★★★★ ☐
Easy crack and slab moves, then thin cranks up a steep seam. Quality.

❻ Name Unknown 5.11c ★★ ☐
Fun climbing up and around a block leads to a mellow finish. The start faces upriver.

❼ Name Unknown 5.10d ★★ ☐
Start on a heart-shaped flake, moving left to a cruxy reach with small feet. Easy edges bring you to a final difficult move in the upper bulge.

❽ Sidewinder 5.11a ★★ ☐
A quality crack in a sea of sport climbs. Tends to be

a little dirty, but the steep jamming makes this climb well worth seeking out.

❾ Jungle Fever 5.11b ★★★ ☐
Another heavily-chalked, high-quality 5.11. An easy pillar leads to steep gastons and layaways. The final bulge can be tackled on the right (easiest), up the middle (hardest), or out left (not too easy, but not too hard).

❿ Torrid Zone 5.12a ★★★ ☐
Wahoo! Some steep 5.12 jug pulling! An outstanding line up hand-swallowing flakes. Powerful (some say reachy) crux section.

⓫ Havana Smack 5.13a ★★★ ☐
Burly, steep climbing. Easier than *The Heathen*, but not by much. Pumpy edges lead to a strenuous sequence near the top.

The following three routes are not shown in the photo but are easily found 25 yards to the left of Havana Smack. *Don't let the lack of chalk steer you away, these are among the best routes at the Northern Point*

⓬ Name Unknown 5.10c/d ★★★ ☐
A chossy start, but the rest of the climb is solid and fun on edges and pockets.

⓭ The Four Nymphs 5.12b ★★★ ☐
Shares the same choss start as the previous route. Stopper technical section at mid-height.

⓮ Sidewalk Café 5.11c ★★★ ☐
A cruiser start leads to a no-hands rest, allowing you time to figure out how you're going to get through the committing crux edge traverse. Great variety of holds and moves on a nice arete.

11
LOWER GORGE

9 mins

68 routes

5.6- 5.7 5.8 5.9 5.10 5.11 5.12 5.13 5.14

sun a.m.

all day shade

DON'T MISS	
Catalyst 5.12b	☐
Dark Star 5.12a	☐
White Trast 5.12a	☐
Try To Be Hip 5.12a	☐
The Pearl 5.11b	☐
Cry of the Poor 5.11a	☐
Pure Palm 5.11a	☐
Last Chance 5.10c	☐
Wildfire 5.10b	☐
Badfinger 5.10b	☐
Cornercopia 5.10b	☐
Gruff 5.10a	☐
Cruel Sister 5.10a	☐

The basalt columns of the Lower Gorge are 'paradise found' for those seeking a break from the tweaky pockets and crossly edges of Smith Rock proper. Down in the Lower Gorge it's all about smooth jams, blank stems, and improbable arêtes. The setting is blissfully natural; the steel-gray walls line the banks of the Crooked River with none of the trampled/manicured crag bases of the Dihedrals or Morning Glory Wall. Adding to the beauty of the place is the amazing lack of climbers due to, well, the fact that trad climbing in the Lower Gorge has never been as *chic* as sport climbing at Smith Rock's frontside crags. That and that the best climbing is in the 5.10 and up zone, with nothing harder than 5.12, keeping away both the masses of beginners and big-digit redpointers. Too bad for them, great for everyone else.

The vast majority of the climbing is gear-protected cracks and corners, but there is also a healthy smattering of bolted arêtes and stem boxes. Almost every trad pitch in the Lower Gorge requires the same standard gear rack (i.e. TCUs, Friends, and nuts). Gear exceptions will be noted when needed (e.g. "gotta have RPs for the crux"), otherwise just use a general rack of small and medium-sized gear.

Another blessing of the Lower Gorge is that it gets tons of shade—typically losing the sun before mid-day. Even in August when just about everything at Smith is too hot to climb, you'll find good temps and a light breeze in the Lower Gorge.

Oh, and one more little secret about the Lower Gorge— save for the two-minute granny stroll to the Northern Point, it has the shortest approach of any climbing at Smith Rock. From the parking lot at the end of Crooked River road walk directly east to the rim and then follow a trail along the rim (heading upstream) for a couple hundred yards (past the ranger house) to a steep scramble. Once the angle of the scramble lessens, hike upstream through the boulder talus, aiming for the first major buttress, the Wildfire Wall.

Heidi Wirtz on *Pure Palm* 5.11a (next page)

WILDFIRE WALL

The highest concentration of quality lines is found here. This wall is absolutely stacked with classics. If you have only one day to climb at the Lower Gorge, this is the spot to hit.

1 Wildfire 5.10b ★★★★ ☐
The namesake route of the cliff, this line is as sweet as they come, marred only slightly by an awkward, cruxy start in a tight corner. After that, though, it's perfect hands and a little bit of fingers to the anchor.

2 La Vie Dansante 5.11d ★★ ☐
French for "The Dancing Life," this route should've been called "The Dancing Deadly Groundfall." You'd be psycho to try and lead this virtually unprotected seam. Best bet is to toprope it off of *Wildfire's* anchors.

3 Crime Wave 5.11b ★★ ☐
Another runout 5.11, though not nearly as dangerous as *La Vie Dansante*. Hard down low and a second crux up high. Numerous rests offer a respite from the techy stems and edges. Rarely led as most everyone just topropes it off of *Gruff's* anchors.

4 Gruff 5.10a ★★★★ ☐
Classic jamming. Can start directly on thin fingers or traverse in on the flake. Sinker locks to a cruxy thin hands section at mid-height. Pumpy for the grade.

5 Rim Job 5.10a ★★★ ☐
Lots of good face rails keep the difficulties in check—just when you start getting pumped or sketched a bucket appears. Not nearly as continuous as *Gruff*.

6 Iron Cross 5.11b ★★ ☐
Another runout 5.11, basically unleadable after the pin was pulled at the blank stemming crux. Can easily toprope it from the anchors on *Badfinger*.

7 Neutral Zone 5.11a ★★ ☐
Easily identified by the dual wide cracks in a chimney/stem box that taper to a crux finger crack around a bulge. Enduro to the top.

8 Badfinger 5.10b ★★★★ ☐
Bad ass! A mega-classic line out bulges, the second being the crux. Continuous and pumpy.

9 Soft Touch 5.10d ★ ☐
A decent line marred (again) by a severely runout start. Botch it before you get to mid-height and you'll for sure deck out. Forget leading this nightmare and simply toprope it off off *Badfinger's* anchor.

10 On The Road 5.11a ★★★★ ☐
One of the sweetest 5.11s at Smith. Hard and funky down low. A second crux kicks in at the bulge midway up before the crack kicks back to cruiser hands. You might consider bringing an extra big hands piece for the last bit.

11 Edge Of The Road 5.12b ★★ ☐
A cool toprope of the arête to the left of *On The Road*. Cryptic and funky the whole way.

12 Titus 5.9 ★★ ☐
A rare Lower Gorge offwidth that is very rarely done. Bring plenty of jumbo cams to deal with this wideness.

13 Split Decision 5.12a ★★ ☐
Yet another one time bold lead relegated to toprope status after the four crux pins were pulled. Technical and thin. Can rig a TR by traversing in from the anchors on *Pure Palm*, but it's not really worth the effort.

14 Pure Palm 5.11a ★★★★ ☐
A classic stem box with virtually no holds. Nonstop calf-pumping stemming and palming. Just as you get to within spitting distance of anchors a final holdless crux hits.

15 Cornercopia 5.10b ★★★★ ☐
A much easier version of *Pure Palm*. Starts with a cruxy bolted section of climbing before leading into a fun stemming. Like *Pure Palm*, there is a final hard bit of insecure climbing directly below the anchor.

16 Name Unknown 5.12a ★★ ☐
Technical climbing that branches off of *Cornercopia* at the roof down low. Sustained and cryptic.

17 Teachers In Space 5.11 ★★ ☐
A good-looking thin crack that gets little to no traffic due to its runout nature on micro nuts. Delicate moves with testy gear placements.

18 Bold Line 5.10c ★ ☐
Starts below the three floating columns looming 50 feet off the deck. After a simple bit of stemming and jamming, step right and bust through the column's roof.

19 Passover 5.10c ★ ☐
Instead of stepping right on *Bold Line*, move up and left out the farthest left column's roof. Watch the rope drag.

20 Resusitation 5.12b/c ★★★ ☐
One of the hardest sport routes in the Lower Gorge. Sustained and technical, especially at the fourth bolt where you'll typically find a bail biner.

WILDFIRE WALL (LEFT)

㉑ White Trash 5.12a ★★★★

Awesome face climbing requiring the full arsenal of technical skills and a superb steep finish. Starts off of a giant flake leaning against the wall. Involved edge climbing leads to the technical crux at the fifth bolt — delicate stems in a tight corner or powerful, reachy slaps out to the arête. Skip the first set of anchors and continue up amazing 5.10 bucket hauling out the multiple roofs and bulges. Wild position up high. 70-meter rope required to lower from upper anchors.

㉒ Lion Of Judah 5.11d ★★

A stout stemming testpiece with an odd-job start. Begin by stick clipping the first bolt above the roof. Then traverse in from the left facing a jumbo ground-skirting swing if you botch it early. You can also skirt the roof on its right but then it's 12b (called *Judah Direct*), super cryptic and powerful, and requires that you stick clip the first two bolts. Above all this starting nonsense is a cool, continuous stemming corner.

㉓ Cry Of The Poor 5.11a ★★★★

A super classic line just to the left of *Lion Of Judah's* roof. A touch hard right off the go with a funky section getting off the big rail. After that it's varied and pumpy moves. If 11a is your grade, you gotta do this route.

㉔ Just Say Yes 5.12a ★★★

A long and involved voyage of edges. The business is at the top but the opening sequence is no path. Starts on funky bulbous rock but quickly turns right onto smooth bullet stone.

㉕ Out Of Darkness 5.11a ★★★

Shares same start as *Just Say Yes* but goes straight up the deceptively hard corner. At the hanging column's roof, clip a bolt and bust up and right, encountering a final crux right below the traverse to the anchor.

㉖ Try To Be Hip 5.12a ★★★★

If 12a is within your limit, you absolutely have to do this awesome line of continuous edges and sidepulls. Classic as they come. Start up *Out Of Darkness* but after 20 feet step left around the arête and on to the face. There are a few good shakes before and after the hardest bits. Harder than *White Trash.*

㉗ Jessie's Line 5.11b ★

Nothing special here — just another of the Lower Gorge's runout, scary 5.11 corners that no one does. Sketch gear down low combined with a funky start (can you say "groundfall"?) keep just about everyone off of this otherwise quality corner. If you do manage to scrape your way past the doomsday start, be sure you have a big cam for up high. You can also swing over from the *Try To Be Hip* anchors and enjoy a stress-free toprope.

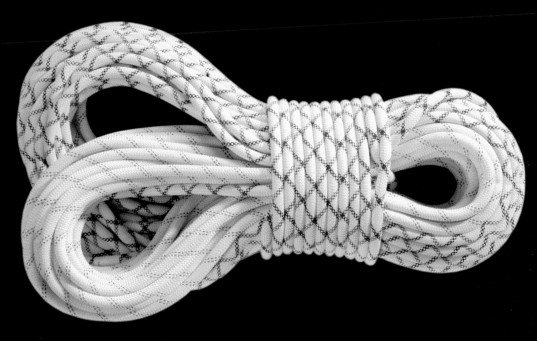

THE RIGHT ROPE

Daunting exposure, desperate redpoints, punishing off-widths, delicate verglas – no worries, with your new Sterling, you have the right rope. Sterling spent many climbing seasons developing a whole new line of dynamic climbing ropes and improving our trademark DryCore™. The result: the right rope for your next climbing adventure. Our new Marathon™ line has the same ultra durable sheath, but a more supple hand. Our Evolution™ line has been redesigned for high performance: lighter with lower impact forces, for those grueling redpoints, committing alpine lines, or trad routes. When faced with endless amounts of fixing, hauling, and rapping, consider our workhorse static lines–the SuperStatic™ and HTP Static™. Whatever corner of the world you're going to, take the right rope.

MARATHON. EVOLUTION. NITRO. SUPERSTATIC. HTP STATIC.
The right ropes for all your climbing endeavors.

Engineered. Tested. Proven.

WWW.STERLINGROPE.COM

CATWALK CLIFF

Found just a touch upstream from Wildfire Wall, this section of cliff is top heavy with classic cracks and light on clip-ups. Fifteen feet above the gurgling Crooked River the trail narrows to the width of a catwalk for a few precarious steps—stumble here and you'll get mangled for sure. Fortunately the climbing begins after the catwalk, but you still need to be mindful of your gear sprawl at the crag base otherwise you might find out that your pack doesn't float.

❶ Name Unknown 5.11c ★★
Just after scooting across the catwalk is this long sport route. Lots of bolts on sweet stone with the line wrapping around an arête down low.

❷ Prometheus 5.10c ★★★
Quality jamming in a stem box. Up high the crux (and the pump) kicks in.

❸ Northern Lights 5.11d ★★
Another technical sport climb that is definitely stout for the grade—especially around the 4th and 5th bolts where the features peter out.

❹ Last Chance 5.10c ★★★★
Mega classic finger crack in an open book. Just keeps getting better and better the higher you climb. A must-do for any 5.10 climber.

❺ Strike Force 5.12a ★
The crux start around a roof keeps most climbers off this rig—not because it's hard (it is, but that ain't the reason) but due to the ancient *Lost Arrow* pin protecting the moves. Blow the moves and the pin could very likely pull, sending you bouncing off into the Crooked River. The rest of climbing is heads up 5.11 but at least you can get some gear in.

❻ Silent Holocaust 5.11c ★★
Unlike *Strike Force*, this climb's opening crux had its jingus pins removed and replaced with bomber bolts. Wow, what a brilliant idea! Replacing crap pins for good bolts—who'da thought such progressive ideas could ever be implemented at Smith Rock? Too bad this sort of replacement is the exception and not the rule. After cruxing through the two tasty bolts, stem through cruiser climbing before traversing right to *Strike Force's* anchors.

❼ Name Unknown 5.11c ★★★
This sport climb is the likely reason for *Silent Holocaust's* retro bolting since it shares the same start.

After pulling the opening roof move up the corner for 10 feet and then step left onto the face. Save some juice for the final roof up high.

❽ Spiritual Warfare 5.11a ★★★
Stem and jam your way up the dueling wide cracks and then punch it through three bulges, the highest one being the hardest. Bring a couple of extra hand-sized pieces for the first half of wide crack.

❾ The Pearl 5.11b ★★★★
An awesome pitch with multiple cruxes and varied moves. It's not as runout as it looks—the moves are thin but the gear is plentiful and bomber. A must-do 5.11 that's super pumpy, especially through the lay-back and bulge sections.

❿ Nuclear 5.11d ★★
The crusty pins on this route scare away most takers. Start in a tight stem box with a bolt and then dice up insecure stems fishing in small nuts and clipping the dodgy pins leading in to a stout section of blank stone right below the roof. Traverse left around the roof up high and into more thin moves. Like just about every pitch in the Lower Gorge that has shitty fixed gear, if the pins were replaced this would be a very popular climb.

⓫ Full Court Press 5.12a ★★★
Non-stop cruxy climbing on edges. Lots of chances to cop mini-rests—if you know how to work'em. Shares the same finish as *Nuclear*.

⓬ Baby Fit 5.11c ★★
Starts in a right-facing mini-corner to the right of less-than-bullet gray rock. As the crack deadens move left onto the face and clip a ancient pin, then move back up and right (crux). Easily toproped from *Name Unknown's* anchors to the left.

⓭ Name Unknown 5.11c ★★★
Though once scabby and sandy, this route's start has cleaned up nicely. Begin up gray (and still somewhat sandy) honeycombed rock. The difficulties slowly increase until a stout bit of edging near the 6th and 7th bolts—where *Bat Flake* is temptingly close. Stemming over to the flake and coping a rest knocks the grade down by a letter grade or two.

⓮ Bat Flake 5.10a ★
Hello, nasty! A really dirty crack on sandy rock out a roof, leads to another roof that is bypassed on the right. The flake on the upper section is the only really good climbing on the whole pitch. Can finish on *Name Unknown's* anchor (more direct) or traverse left to *Satan's Awaiting's* anchor (original finish).

⓯ Satan's Awaiting 5.11a ★
Shares the same scrappy start as *Bat Flake* but pulls the second roof on its left side and into thin jams and stems. Good stuff above the roof but the gross start detracts from the overall value.

CATWALK CLIFF (LEFT)

⑯ Rising Star 5.11a ★
Another line that is doomed by the shitty gray rock down low. That and the thin, runout nature of the initial section getting up to the first roof. Above the second roof is great stone and thin finger locks. Shares anchor with *Satan's Awaiting*.

⑰ White Dwarf 5.11b ★
A runout nightmare that no one does. It's good climbing with techy stems but gear down low is few and far between. Best just to toprope this from *Satan's Awaiting's* anchor.

⑱ Night Shift 5.11b ★★★
A continuously difficult corner that is a bit of sandbag. Expect stout moves with small nuts for protection. If you're leading head is dialed in, this beautiful corner is worth a shot.

⑲ Ground Zero 5.10d ★★★
Likely the biggest sandbag in the Lower Gorge. A cryptic section of climbing 20 feet up feels a lot like mid-range 5.11—especially if you try to power it and not tech it. Luckily at the crux you have bomber gear right at your face—perfect for dogging through the moves. Above the crux is significantly easier climbing that eventually traverses left to *Quasar's* anchor.

⑳ Quasar 5.10a ★★★
A relatively short pitch with perfect jams. A great warm-up for some of the harder climbing nearby.

㉑ Erogenous Zone 5.10c ★★★
The crux kicks in early just off the beginning ledge. Thin locks with solid gear quickly open up to hand jams. Can reach over to *Quasar's* anchor or continue up for 20 more feet to the upper anchor.

㉒ Blood Clot 5.10b ★★★
A cruiser hand crack with plenty of rests. Take one or two large cams to protect the crack's wider finish.

㉓ Crack-A-No-Go 5.11b ★★★
The first half of this outstanding crack is thin and pumpy with some interesting sections of committing layaways. The upper bit is easy big hands (bring a large cam). Unlike its Yosemite namesake, this pitch takes good gear exactly where you need it.

㉔ Cruel Sister 5.10a ★★★★
One of the best 5.10 cracks at Smith. Sustained jams are perfect all the way to the anchor on this clean open book crack, save for a bit of rattly big hands up high (make sure to bring a large cam or two).

㉕ Catalyst (a.k.a. Child Abuse) 5.12b ★★★★
An old school toprope that got bolted and renamed *Child Abuse*. The original name may have changed but the climbing is as good as ever. Cryptic slaps and edges up dual arêtes. Very unique climbing makes this a Lower Gorge classic.

㉖ Taxtor 5.9 ★★
If you need an offwidth fix, this is your hook up. Fists to chicken wings to chimneying. Bring the full quiver of large cams for this big daddy.

㉗ Southern Cross 5.11a ★★
An underappreciated pen-book corner due to the lack of protection down low. Basically it's another should-be-a-classic route that is hamstrung by its runout nature. A pin used to protect the thin part of the lower section, but has since been pulled. Even with the pin this was a head's up lead, now it's basically a solo through the first 30 feet.

photography by ben moon   moonfoto.com

STAR WALL

A stacked wall about 100 yards upstream from the Catwalk Cliff. The start of the cliff is easily identified by two newly bolted (circa 2005) sport/trad climbs first encountered as you descend a small vine-covered hill. The wall has great selection of both trad and sport climbs, the best being in the 5.11+ to 5.12 range.

1 Name Unknown 5.11? ★
A newish sport climb that requires a couple of smaller cams for the crack start. The clean face tips back to a licheny slab up high.

2 Last Days 5.10a ★★★
A shortish but sweet hand crack. Clean rock with straight-in jams make this a great lead for those breaking into 5.10 cracks.

3 Name Unknown 5.11? ★
Another newish sport/trad line, this one starting off just to the left of *Last Days* on the column's face. A hard section down low yields to a sloping ledge and easy stemming and crack climbing above. Bring a couple small to medium pieces for the upper crack.

8 Cry Of The Gerbil 5.12b ★★★
A stout test of technical stemming down low on so-so rock. Up high it's pumper edges with few rests. One of the harder sport pitches in the Lower Gorge.

9 Dark Star 5.12a ★★★★
An absolutely classic corner. One of the best 5.12a pitches at Smith Rock. Thin crack and stem moves lead into the upper crux section, protected by four solid pins. There are two ways to do the crux: either stem in the corner or slap out on the arête—neither is easy.

10 Neutron Star 5.12a ★★★
A great line rarely led due to the shitty knifeblades for gear up high. Fortunately it's easily toproped from *Dark Star's* anchor. Thin, technical, and pumpy the entire way, though crux is at the bolt at the mini roof at one-third height.

DARK STAR: "An absolutely classic corner. One of the best 5.12a pitches at Smith ..."

4 St. Paddee's Day 5.10a ★
A wide crack few climbers bother with. A little dirty as well. Bring plenty of big cams for the opening wideness.

5 Turning Point 5.10a ★★
No, the lower part doesn't look good—and it's wide. Once through the big stuff, though (which obviously requires a couple large cams), you get to enjoy a cool sequence pulling pumpy layaways out a bulge on fingers. The climbing above the bulge is easy and ends with a leftwards traverse to *Mantra's* anchor.

6 Lethal Dose 5.11a ★
Thin and crumbly rock down low combined with run-outs on RPs doesn't make for a wildly popular route. After the spookfest start you'll be sinking solid jams to the anchor.

7 Mantra 5.10a ★★★
A great warm-up for the harder lines at the Star Wall. After a crunchy start a few hard finger lock moves yield to stellar hands.

11 Jonny and the Melonheads 5.12b ★★
Another sweet line with ridiculously bad pins. If someone ever replaced the pins with bolts, this would be a four-star classic. If you want to lead it, be sure to bring plenty of thin gear and a solid head for runouts on insecure stems.

12 Morning Star 5.10c ★★★
Just to the left of where some yahoo etched a one-foot-tall outline of a climber is this excellent and varied crack. Another great warm-up for the harder pitches nearby. A bit awkward at midheight and pumpy all the way.

13 Name Unknown 5.12a ★★
A fun sport route that up high comes annoying close to climbers on *Morning Star.* Cruxy at the third and fourth bolts.

14 Night Crossing 5.11b ★
Does a broken crack littered with bushes sound good? Well, then, boot up. Otherwise avoid in favor of the Star Wall's much better routes.

GRADED LIST OF TRADITIONAL ROUTES

5.4
☐ Left Slab Crack ★ 40

5.5
☐ Right Slab Crack ★★ 40

5.6
☐ Cinnamon Slab ★★★★ 40

5.7
☐ Bookworm ★★★★ 48
☐ Pioneer Route (5.7 A0) ★★★ 66
☐ Friday's Jinx ★★★ 38
☐ Rabbit Stew ★★★ 48
☐ Lycopodophyta ★★★ 48
☐ Cinnamon Toast 40

5.8
☐ West Face Variation (5.8 A0) ★★★★ 64
☐ Lion's Jaw ★★★ 35
☐ Pack Animal ★★★ 38
☐ Cliff Dwelling Crack ★★ 60

5.9
☐ Moonshine Dihedral ★★★★ 46
☐ Sundown ★★★ 60
☐ Solar ★★ 26
☐ Toys in the Attic ★★ 55
☐ Titus ★★ 72
☐ Taxtor ★★ 78

5.10a
☐ Karate Crack ★★★★ 44
☐ New Testament ★★★★ 54
☐ Tezlar ★★★★ 61
☐ Gruff ★★★★ 72
☐ Cruel Sister ★★★★ 78
☐ Tale of Two Shitties ★★★ 60
☐ Rim Job ★★★ 72
☐ Quasar ★★★ 78
☐ Last Days ★★★ 80
☐ Mantra ★★★ 80
☐ Toy Blocks ★★ 55
☐ Chimney de Chelly ★★ 60
☐ Turning Point ★★ 80
☐ Bat Flake ★ 76
☐ St. Paddee's Day ★ 80

5.10b
☐ Zebra/Zion ★★★★ 34
☐ Pack Animal Direct ★★★★ 38
☐ Wildfire ★★★★ 72
☐ Badfinger ★★★★ 72
☐ Cornercopia ★★★★ 72
☐ Crack of Infinity ★★★ 38
☐ Hesitation Blues ★★★ 55
☐ Blood Clot ★★★ 78

5.10c
☐ Last Chance ★★★★ 76
☐ Calamity Jam ★★★ 38
☐ Prometheus ★★★ 76
☐ Erogenous Zone ★★★ 78
☐ Morning Star ★★★ 80
☐ Sandbag ★★ 38
☐ Child's Play ★★ 55
☐ Bold Line ★ 72
☐ Passover ★ 72

5.10d
☐ Ground Zero ★★★ 78
☐ Soft Touch ★ 72

5.11a
☐ Lion's Chair ★★★★ 34
☐ On the Road ★★★★ 72
☐ Cry of the Poor ★★★★ 74
☐ Desolation Row ★★★ 60
☐ Out of Darkness ★★★ 74
☐ Spiritual Warfare ★★★ 76
☐ Sidewinder ★★ 69
☐ Neutral Zone ★★ 72
☐ Southern Cross ★★ 78
☐ Satan's Awaiting ★ 76
☐ Rising Star ★ 78
☐ Lethal Dose ★ 80

5.11b
☐ Wartley's Revenge ★★★★ 53
☐ Golgotha ★★★★ 54
☐ Pearl, The ★★★★ 76
☐ Karot Tots ★★★ 44

Night Shift ★★★ 78
☐ Night Shift ★★★ 78
☐ Crack-A-No-Go ★★★ 78
☐ Cocaine Crack ★★ 26
☐ Crime Wave ★★ 72
☐ Iron Cross ★★ 72
☐ Jessie's Line ★ 74
☐ White Dwarf ★ 78
☐ Night Crossing ★ 80
☐ Shoes of the Fisherman 52

5.11c
☐ Silent Holocaust ★★ 76
☐ Baby Fit ★★ 76

5.11d
☐ Sunshine Dihedral ★★★★ 46
☐ Astro Monkey ★★★★ 64
☐ Rising Expectations ★★★★ 66
☐ Minas Morgul ★★ 60
☐ La Vie Dansante ★★ 72
☐ Nuclear ★★ 76

5.11
☐ Teachers in Space ★★ 72

5.12a
☐ West Face of Monkey Face ★★★★ 65
☐ North Face of Monkey Face ★★★★ 66
☐ Dark Star ★★★★ 80
☐ Neutron Star ★★★ 80
☐ Catastrophic Crack ★★ 38
☐ Split Decision ★★ 72
☐ Strike Force ★ 76

5.12b
☐ Sheer Trickery ★★★ 65
☐ Edge of the Road ★★ 72
☐ Jonny and the Melonheads ★★ 80

5.13a
☐ Double Stain ★★ 55

5.13d
☐ East Face of Monkey Face ★★★★ 66

GRADED LIST OF SPORT ROUTES

5.5
- Night Flight ★★★ 40

5.6
- Easy Reader ★★★ 40

5.7
- Bunny Face ★★★★ 48
- Dancer ★★★ 55
- Purple Headed Warrior, The ★★ 26

5.8
- 5 Gallon Buckets ★★★★ 35
- Hop on Pop ★★★ 38
- Lichen It ★★★ 40
- Ginger Snap ★★★ 40
- Jete ★★★ 55
- Peanut Brittle ★★ 38
- Hissing Llamas ★★ 58

5.9
- 9 Gallon Buckets ★★★★ 32
- Cry Baby ★★★★ 40
- Outsiders, The ★★★ 35
- Phone Call From Satan ★★ 26
- Snuffy Smith ★★ 38
- Ancylostoma ★★ 48
- Helium Woman ★★ 48
- Revelations ★★ 54
- Rodney's Chocolate Frosted 40

5.10a
- Light on the Path ★★★ 35
- Pop Goes the Nubbin ★★★ 38
- Irreverence ★★★ 54
- Phoenix ★★★ 58
- Caffeine Free ★★ 26
- Tuff It Out ★★ 38
- Captain Xenolith ★★ 48
- Nightingale's on Vacation ★★ 54
- Drill'em and Fill'em ★★ 58
- Down's Syndrome ★★ 60
- Cosmos ★★ 61
- Tater Tots ★ 45
- Unknown ★ 55
- Methuselah's Column 48

5.10b
- Barbeque the Pope ★★★★ 54
- Screaming Yellow Zonkers ★★★★ 60
- Chicken McNuggets ★★★ 26
- Gumby ★★★ 34
- Wedding Day ★★★ 46
- JT's Route ★★★ 58
- Equine-imity ★★ 39
- Double Trouble ★★ 55
- Sundancer ★ 39

5.10c
- 9 Gallon Bucks... (extension) ★★★★ 32
- Lion Zion ★★★ 34
- Morning Sky ★★★ 34
- Deep Impact ★★ 27
- Tammy Baker's Face ★★ 35
- Unknown ★★ 38
- Massive Luxury Overdose ★★ 61

5.10c/d
- Unknown ★★★ 69

5.10d
- Headless Horseman ★★★★ 39
- Moons of Pluto ★★★★ 60
- Reason to Be ★★★ 60
- Powder Up the Nose ★★ 27
- Unknown ★★ 38
- Fred on Air ★★ 58
- Unknown ★★ 69
- Trivial Pursuit ★ 45
- Cows In Agony ★ 60

5.11a
- Magic Light ★★★★ 32
- Bad Moon Rising ★★★★ 60
- Woman in the Meadow ★★★★ 69
- Limbo ★★★★ 69
- Pure Palm ★★★★ 72
- Bound In Bogota ★★ 27
- Armageddon ★★ 27
- Cool Ranch Flavor ★★ 30
- Blasphemy ★★ 54
- Zebra Direct ★ 34
- Overnight Sensation ★ 55
- When Llamas Bolt ★ 58
- Freshly Squeezed 45

5.11b
- Toxic ★★★★ 23
- Vomit Launch ★★★★ 26
- Overboard ★★★★ 32
- Monkey Space ★★★★ 64
- Cat Scan ★★★ 35
- Jungle Fever ★★★ 69
- Popism ★★ 38
- Unknown ★★ 38
- Equus ★★ 39
- Attic Antics ★★ 55
- License to Bolt ★★ 58
- Shake 'N Flake ★ 27

5.11c
- Bloodshot ★★★ 27
- Moondance ★★★ 46
- Sidewalk Café ★★★ 69
- Unknown ★★★ 76
- Unknown ★★★ 76
- Middle Aged Vandals ★★ 46
- Unknown ★★ 38
- Unknown ★★ 69
- Unknown ★★ 76
- Private Trust ★ 55
- Drug Nasty 64

5.11c/d
- Ring of Fire ★★ 55

5.11d
- Up For Grabs ★★★★ 23
- Zebra Seam ★★★ 34
- Moving in Stereo ★★★ 64
- Slow Burn ★★ 44
- Rawhide ★★ 52
- Heresy ★★ 53
- Lion of Judah ★★ 74
- Northern Lights ★★ 76
- Deep Splash ★ 52

5.11
- Unknown ★ 80
- Unknown ★ 80

5.12a

Power Dive	★★★★	44
Take a Powder	★★★★	46
Heinous Cling Start	★★★★	46
Dreamin'	★★★★	52
White Trash	★★★★	74
Try to Be Hip	★★★★	74
The Blade	★★★	26
Freebase	★★★	26
Latin Lover	★★★	45
Spank the Monkey	★★★	66
Torrid Zone	★★★	69
Just Say Yes	★★★	74
Full Court Press	★★★	76
Panic Attack	★★	54
Juniper Face	★★	60
Shadow of Doubt	★★	60
Unknown	★★	72
Unknown	★★	80
Highway to Hell	★	22
The Flat Earch		46

5.12a/b

Peepshow	★★★	45

5.12b

Magic Light (extension)	★★★★	32
Crossfire	★★★★	44
Firing Line	★★★★	44
Latest Rage	★★★★	44
Vision	★★★★	48
Catalyst	★★★★	78
Crack Babies	★★★	27
The Four Nymphs	★★★	69
Cry of the Gerbil	★★★	80
Energy Crisis	★★	32
Watts Tots	★★	45
Boy Prophet	★★	52
Rabid	★	27
Shiva	★	69

5.12b/c

Resusitation	★★★	72

5.12c

Quickening, The	★★★★	23
Karate Wall	★★★★	44
Last Waltz	★★★★	46
Fully Heinous	★★★★	47
Chain Reaction	★★★★	47
Go Dog Go	★★★★	48
Da Kine Corner	★★★	30

Choss In America	★★★	34
Doritos	★★	30
Powder In Your Eyes	★★	46
Pose Down	★★	65
Close Shave	★★	66
Nacho Cheese	★	30
Made in the Rain	★★	69
La Shootist	★	52

5.12d

Kings of Rap	★★★★	30
Sketch Pad	★★	32
Magalithic	★★	66
Dandy Line	★	34

5.13a

Churning in the Wake	★★★★	30
Churning Sky	★★★★	30
Darkness at Noon	★★★★	47
The Backbone	★★★★	66
Taco Chips	★★★	30
Heathen, The	★★★	69
Havana Smack	★★★	69
Choke on This	★★	52
Mane Line	★	32

5.13a/b

Time's Up	★★★	26
Oxygen	★★★	30

5.13b

Aggro Monkey	★★★★	22
Slit Your Wrist	★★★★	26
Churning in the Ozone	★★★★	30
French Connection	★★★★	46
Scene of the Crime	★★★	23
Waste Case	★★★	30
Power	★★	26
Smooth Boy	★★	52
Bum Rush the Show	★★	55
Evil Sister		47

5.13b/c

Rude Boys	★★★★	52

5.13c

Lucky Pigeon	★★★	22
Mama Docus	★★	23
Disposable Heroes	★★	23
Rude Femmes	★★	52
Crime Wave	★	23

5.13c/d

Vicious Fish	★★★★	30

5.13d

White Wedding	★★★★	22
Spank the Monkey Extension	★★★	66
Jam Master Jay	★★	30

5.14a

Bad Man	★★★★	22
To Bolt or Not To Be	★★★★	46
Scarface	★★★★	52
Villain	★★★	22
Mr. Yuck	★★★	26
Chemical Ali	★★★	52
Repeat Offender	★★	22

5.14b

Just Do It	★★★★	66

5.14c

Shock and Awe	★★★★	22

5.14?

White Heat	★	30

INDEX